the mothercare guide to

TRAVELLING WITH CHILDREN

Sarah Litvinoff

Conran Octopus

Project editor	Jane O'Shea
Editor	Carole McGlynn
Project assistant	Debora Robertson
Art editor	Christine Wood
Production	Shane Lask
Illustrations	Jenny Norton
Jacket photograph	Andy Cox

First published in 1989 by
Conran Octopus Limited
37 Shelton Street
London WC2H 9HN

Copyright © 1989 Conran Octopus

All rights reserved. No part of this book may be reproduced, stored in a retrieval system or transmitted in any form or by any means, electronic, electrostatic, magnetic tape, mechanical, photocopying, recording or otherwise, without the prior permission in writing of the publisher.

ISBN 1 85029 168 3

Typeset by Bookworm Typesetting, Manchester
Printed by Eagle Press plc, Scotland

CONTENTS

Introduction **4**

What kind of holiday? **6**

Planning **16**

What to take **24**

Travel equipment **28**

All you need for your journey **31**

On the move **39**

Safety on holiday **49**

Health and first aid **53**

Useful addresses **62**

Index **63**

INTRODUCTION

Children make a holiday: there is nothing so touching as a child's face glowing with pleasure and excitement at what a new environment has to offer. Family holidays give an added dimension to family life – a time when you can all be together without having to rush, in a place where you can forget work, school and domestic responsibilities. This time is precious. It is hard to make space to give everyone proper attention in a normal week, so holidays become the best time for really appreciating the togetherness of family life.

Children are by nature curious, and even those who cling to the familiar will be fascinated with what a holiday in a new place has to offer. This does not have to mean going abroad: a different part of Britain where there is countryside instead of town, or sea instead of roads, can be as exciting as the most exotic foreign location.

Holidays provide the golden memories that punctuate family life and that take up more than their fair share of the photograph album. Even a young child who seems to have no conscious memory of a wonderful holiday will have drawn the benefit of family togetherness, and older children will remember with glee perhaps the very things you would rather forget – disasters have a way of becoming funny in time. It seems that my daughter's favourite holiday memories are of things going wrong: the holiday spoilt by torrential rain; the time that all the fireworks for an evening celebration went off at once and we had to dive for cover during the mad five minutes when they whizzed, banged and sparked; the occasion when, issued with the wrong railway tickets, we were under threat of being thrown off the train in the middle of the night. Who can say what is going to make a holiday perfect – or, at least, memorable?

But the drawback is that travelling with children can be difficult. Even quite short journeys can be gruelling for a small child who is not used to having to sit still, and making sure that everything goes smoothly when you arrive at the other end involves a good deal of preparation and foresight. This may be one of the reasons that holidays figure so high in the scale of events that cause stress levels to rise.

There is certainly no need to feel that having children marks the end of your adventuring life. You can take the children with you on almost any kind of holiday. Experienced travellers say that children's fresh approach and original way of seeing things makes them ideal travelling companions.

This book helps you plan your holiday with the children in mind, so that you can do your best to make sure that you all enjoy yourselves. You may even find the planning and preparation fun too – it becomes a part of the holiday, in which the whole family joins.

There are just four golden rules for trouble-free travel:

> ▶ **Be prepared** If you plan carefully and think out all the potential problems well before the holiday begins, you are most likely to make a success of it. This means choosing your destination with care, finding out everything you need to know about it, and packing all that is essential to your family's well-being.
> ▶ **Stay calm** Once you have planned, packed and are off, a calm, philosophical attitude from you affects all the family. Remember: this is fun, not work, and the more relaxed and leisurely the pace, the more everyone will feel in the holiday mood.
> ▶ **Be flexible** If you are able to plan your timing, make sure nothing is rushed. Be guided by the moods and needs of your children. Travelling itself is a strain for little ones, who may behave uncharacteristically. Let them sleep when they are tired, and give them snacks and drinks when they want them: a well-fed, well-rested child is the best-tempered child.
> ▶ **Enjoy yourself** It's your holiday too, and the more fun you have, the happier your children will be and the better your memories in years to come.

This book is one of a series of Mothercare Guides that covers topics of immediate interest to parents of young children. The books are all fully illustrated and offer clear and straightforward guidance on practical aspects of everyday childcare. The other titles available in the series are listed on the back jacket of this book.

All the information in these books applies equally to male and female children. To reflect this, the pronouns 'he' and 'she' have been used in alternating chapters throughout each book.

WHAT KIND OF HOLIDAY?

Before the children came along your main considerations before you went on holiday were likely to be: what do I really want to do, where would I like to go and can I afford it? But children change your perspective on most things, and not surprisingly holidays look rather different when you are considering the younger members of the family as well. If you are going to enjoy your holiday to the full, your children will have to enjoy it too – and what makes a holiday memorable and fun will change as your children grow older.

This chapter gives a brief run-down of the different kinds of holiday you may be considering, and what the advantages and disadvantages are from the point of view of the children – and, of course, you. If you are new parents then this section is particularly useful, as it gives a brief account of things to consider, which may not even have entered your head before.

It is true that if you are a seasoned traveller and determined to make it work, there really is no kind of holiday you cannot take your children on. But it has to be said that some kinds of holiday are very much more suitable than others with children in tow. If your aim is to relax and gather strength for the rest of the year, you will probably choose one of these. But if holiday means challenge and change to you then you may decide on a more demanding option. Children whose parents take them on unconventional holidays from the beginning often develop a hardy tolerance – as well as a liking – for this kind of travel.

You know the kind of holiday *you* would like. But what's the best choice for your children at different ages?

Type of holiday	Baby	Toddler	Ages 3-5	Ages 5-8	Ages 8-11
Self-catering in Britain	✪✪✪	✪✪✪	✪✪	✪✪	✪✪
Self-catering abroad	✪✪	✪✪	✪✪	✪✪	✪✪
Hotel in Britain	✪	✪	✪	✪	✪✪
Camping and caravans: Britain and abroad	✪	✪	✪✪	✪✪✪	✪✪✪
Package hotel abroad: beach	✪	✪✪	✪✪✪	✪✪✪	✪✪✪
Package hotel abroad: countryside	✪	✪	✪✪	✪✪	✪
Package hotel abroad: city	✪	✪	✪	✪	✪✪
Holiday camp/centre in Britain	✪✪	✪✪	✪✪	✪✪✪	✪✪✪
House-swapping abroad	✪✪	✪✪	✪✪	✪✪	✪✪✪
Activity holiday	✪	✪	✪	✪✪	✪✪✪

✪ poor choice   ✪✪ all right but some drawbacks   ✪✪✪ good choice

SELF-CATERING IN BRITAIN

Self-catering means renting a place for the family to stay in which you do your own cooking and cleaning as you would at home – and which you are expected to leave respectably clean at the end. Some self-catering properties, particularly in holiday complexes, have staff to clean and change beds, etc., but in the greater majority of them you will be expected to do these chores yourself. You will also probably have to take towels and bed linen with you.

The kind of accommodation on offer varies. Many of the properties to rent will be in the country, and therefore quite isolated from the entertainments children might like, although there are some to be found beside the sea. You can find them through companies that specialize in self-catering properties, small ads in the newspaper or regional tourist boards, which usually keep lists.

Choosing to stay in Britain means that you should not have to travel too far from home but it is possible to enjoy a completely different type of environment. And although you may not get the brilliant weather of the continent, the language and the lifestyle are familiar – and favourite television programmes need not be missed. Try to choose a location that is not too isolated if your children are at a sociable age: meeting friends can make a holiday.

Advantages for adults
You can structure your own time and your children's bed- and mealtimes. Because you are self-contained, you don't have to worry about restraining the children's boisterous behaviour. You should have no problems buying your usual baby foods/nappies and no worries about the younger ones having to get used to a drastic change in climate.

Advantages for children
They can behave very much as they would at home. Babies do not need to have their routine unduly disrupted. Friends they make will usually be English-speaking.

Drawbacks for adults
It will be a change but not so much of a holiday if you find you are doing as much work as you normally would at home. But this is not necessary – you can do more easily-prepared or *al fresco* meals, and your partner will be more involved and can share responsibilities.

Drawbacks for children
Older children may be bored if you go to a pretty cottage somewhere without considering the entertainment on offer. It's better for the older ones if you choose a location where there are a number of interesting activities.

SELF-CATERING ABROAD

Choosing a self-catering holiday abroad gives you a foreign holiday at a much lower price than if you stayed in a hotel. The choice of place and type of accommodation is infinite, from cottages in rural settings in France, to an apartment in a Spanish seaside town. Accommodation in a purpose-built holiday complex usually includes use of a pool and entertainment facilities for the children, as well as convenient (but highly-priced) shops, and restaurants if you want to forget cooking for once.

Some tour companies specialize in self-catering properties, or have separate brochures for them. Other properties are advertised privately in newspapers. You will have the choice of simply renting the accommodation itself, and making your own travel arrangements, or buying an all-in 'package' which includes the house, villa or apartment and your flights, or ferry crossing, to get there. The all-inclusive type of holiday is usually priced according to the number of people in your party.

Advantages for adults
It allows the usual flexibility of self-catering with the bonus of an exotic location for holiday atmosphere. If the weather is good you will find you can get away with less cooking than at home, with plenty of barbecues, salads, sandwiches, cheeses and fresh fruit. On the occasions that you eat out rather than cook, you will find children far more welcome in continental restaurants than British ones. Self-catering in a holiday complex often provides some sort of maid service.

Advantages for children
They are not constrained by hotel rules relating to children. Even abroad the food does not have to be 'foreign' if they are picky eaters – you can make the sort of meals they like. Young children will not find language differences a barrier, and may pick up a few foreign words.

Drawbacks for adults
Some foreign countries will not have the baby foods or equipment you have come to rely on, or they may be much more expensive than at home. Health and medical emergencies can be more of a problem far from home if you don't speak the language.

Drawbacks for children
Older children who need to talk to friends may find it lonely if there are no other English speakers of a similar age to themselves.

HOTEL IN BRITAIN

On the whole British hotels do not cater for children, but there is a substantial minority that welcomes them. These are most likely to be sited in the areas that children like best anyway, such as near the sea. The best ones go out of their way to provide facilities and perhaps supervised activities for younger children, as well as a baby-listening or baby-sitting service. It is harder to find a hotel with these qualities that also follows through with a high standard for adults – but there are some, and it is worth looking through the guide books that list them. You should find these in a good newsagent or bookshop.

Advantages for adults
There is no domestic work or cooking to be done. It is reassuring to be in your own country when you have young children, or if any of your children have delicate health. If you choose the right hotel, you have a good chance of enjoying a complete rest.

Advantages for children
Older children like the 'luxury' of hotel rooms. If the hotel welcomes children they can be assured of lots of playmates and activities all on their own doorstep.

Drawbacks for adults
Children are less well tolerated publicly in Britain, and unless you choose a hotel that positively welcomes them, they will have to be well-controlled at mealtimes and may be denied use of the public rooms after certain hours. Unless the hotel caters for children with special activities, lots of time and energy will have to be spent amusing them. Laundry costs are high and it may be difficult to wash and dry your children's clothes – particularly a problem with babies and grubby under-fives.

Drawbacks for children
They must be on reasonably good behaviour while in the hotel, and may have to fit in with the hotel timetable, which can be disruptive for toddlers and annoying for the older ones.

CAMPING AND CARAVANS: BRITAIN AND ABROAD

You have the option of taking your own caravan/camping equipment, or hiring one already set up at the site of your choice. Although the first option gives you the freedom to move from site to site and is the obvious choice if you already have the equipment, it is not recommended unless you are already experienced travellers. The best compromise is to hire for the first holiday or two, and then buy your own equipment once you have found that you all enjoy it. New-style, luxury fixed tents have separate rooms, 'windows', a fridge and even toilets in some cases. Many designated camp-sites are quite sophisticated, especially on the continent, with good facilities such as launderettes, well-maintained showers and swimming pools. The better weather abroad also makes an open-air holiday even more attractive for the whole family.

Both in Britain and abroad, the better the camp-site, and the more facilities there are for children, the more expensive it is. But camping is still a cheaper alternative to renting a self-catering apartment, house or cottage.

Advantages for adults
It is relatively cheap, and has many of the advantages of self-catering. Cooking and eating outdoors can be much more fun than being a slave in the kitchen.

Advantages for children
Most children love the outdoor experience. Even rain – a misery on most holidays – is exciting when it is drumming on the caravan roof or on canvas. There will be lots of other families around, so making friends is easy. Foreign camp-sites often provide a variety of activities for children, including swimming pools.

Drawbacks for adults
Accommodation can be cramped, and you may not like the communal washing facilities. If camping on a popular site you can find that the proximity of other families makes for a noisy and not very restful time. If the weather is bad, you could find it hard work keeping the children fed, amused and in clean, dry clothes.

Drawbacks for children
It is not really suitable for children below the age of two, with all the clothes, nappies and special baby equipment that they need. If your child still wakes frequently at night, he may keep the whole camp-site awake, which could make you rather unpopular.

PACKAGE HOTEL ABROAD: BEACH

Of all foreign holidays this is probably the favourite with children of almost every age, except babies who cannot enjoy the sand, sea and sun. The good weather means children will spend little time cooped up indoors, and a beach offers endless fun for quiet as well as energetic children, without the need for special play equipment. An added bonus is that many hotels by the sea have special facilities for children and supervised play. As a general rule, the larger the hotel the more they will have on offer for young children. Older children will also appreciate a package with supervised sporting activities.

If you are taking a baby, for whom sand will only be an irritant, and the sun too strong, make sure that your hotel has its own pool and pleasant poolside with a shaded area.

Advantages for adults
There is plenty to keep all but small babies amused. There is no cooking or domestic work involved.

Advantages for children
Sea and sand offer endless fun even for the solitary child, and there are usually masses of other children to play with. Boisterous children can rush around and let off steam as much as they like – they are well tolerated on this type of holiday.

Drawbacks for adults
The rooms in package hotels are usually small and you may have to have your child or children sharing with you. If any of your children are sun-sensitive you may have to take it in turns to look after them away from the beach, where there may not be much else to do during the day.

Drawbacks for children
Babies will find hot sun and a sandy environment unpleasant. All fair-skinned children have to be careful in the sun, and may be frustrated by the fact that they can only remain uncovered for a short time each day for at least the first week. Some children may dislike the hotel food.

PACKAGE HOTEL ABROAD: COUNTRYSIDE

These may be less popular with children than beach holidays, though they can offer greater variety for the family as a whole. They can be a particularly good choice off-season – when it's too cold for the beach and conditions are not right for skiing. Inland holiday areas do not always cater for children to the same degree as seaside resorts, but they may offer more opportunities for alternative excursions. Depending on the area you choose, you may be within easy reach of lakes, caves, museums or historic sights – or all of these.

Advantages for adults
The right area will offer a quieter atmosphere than a beach resort and it will be easier to keep young children out of the direct sun if you go in the height of summer. Ski-resorts that want to fill the rooms off-season will usually be well-equipped with pools, saunas and sporting opportunities as well as offering the excitement of mountain scenery.

Advantages for children
There may be a greater variety of amusements, and some children prefer this to a constant diet of sea and sun. An off-season choice usually means that your children are below school age, which means they won't miss communal entertainment facilities in the same way: your company is more important.

Drawbacks for adults
Lack of facilities for children can make it more difficult to keep them entertained.

Drawbacks for children
Depending on the hotel, and the area you choose, it may not be such a good choice for older children who like to be kept amused, with plenty of things to do, and to be with other children.

PACKAGE HOTEL ABROAD: CITY

If you are culturally-inclined, you may prefer to take your foreign holiday in a city where there are places of historic or artistic interest to visit. This is a less appealing holiday to children, though an infant who is still being carried around in a sling will mind least. Older, quiet children, who prefer adult company and share adult interests, and are perhaps shy of their own contemporaries, are likely to welcome this kind of holiday. A compromise is a 'two-centre' holiday in which you spend part of the time by the beach, say, and the rest in a city. This may be a way to please different members of the family.

Advantages for adults
You can see what the city has to offer at your leisure, whereas arranged cultural excursions from a holiday site often involve a long and tedious coach journey, which makes the children restless, and then a structured guided tour at the end. If the children's attention span is short you can make brief 'taster' visits to places of interest, but return to the hotel when you wish. It is a good choice for an 'off-season' holiday.

Advantages for children
Even if the weather is bad, a city is likely to offer alternative entertainment under cover, such as museums, art galleries, cinemas and swimming pools.

Drawbacks for adults
The children have to be taken around with you most of the time, and if they are unwilling or miserable it will spoil your pleasure. Not surprisingly, as city holidays are not a very popular choice for families, city hotels are unlikely to be geared to children, and therefore you won't find much in the way of special facilities, mealtimes or entertainment for children in the hotel. Usually a higher standard of behaviour will be expected from them than at a beach resort.

Drawbacks for children
All but the most quiet and disciplined child is likely to find this kind of holiday restrictive to some extent.

HOLIDAY CAMP/CENTRE IN BRITAIN

Holiday camps have come a long way since the days of *Hi-de-Hi* – they are more sophisticated for adults, while retaining all the features that make them irresistible to children. Accommodation is usually in self-contained chalets or flats. You can choose full-board, half-board, or self-catering – with the last you will usually have a larger chalet. Within the complex there will be a restaurant and bar or club room as well as various other amenities that would normally include a swimming pool, playground and other sports facilities. In recognition of the unstable climate in Britain, more of them are now offering covered and heated pools, with water chutes and wave machines.

In the most comprehensive holiday camps there are non-stop activities throughout the day and evening, with supervised play and sports tuition for the children. Sometimes there will be a mini-funfair with all the rides free. It's no wonder that children love this kind of holiday. In the evenings there is usually entertainment for the adults as well. If you choose a holiday camp purely for the children's sake, but are not particularly keen on what is on offer for yourself, you can use the time while they are supervised during the day to leave the centre and explore the area. A few camps do not welcome babies, but most do, and many have good baby-sitting and nursery facilities; some even have free nappy washing.

Advantages for adults
With the children so happy and well-occupied it is possible for you really to have time to yourselves, and to get a complete rest if that is what you want from your holiday.

Advantages for children
It's a rare child who does not love this kind of holiday, particularly over the age of five. There are endless activities on offer to suit almost every age and kind of child and it is possible for them to make lots of friends.

Drawbacks for adults
If you do not like the community atmosphere and what seems like relentless fun, you can find this type of holiday unrelaxing. It can also be very noisy. You may find the standards of comfort and the quality of the food disappointing, and the accommodation rather cramped.

Drawbacks for children
Almost none – unless your child is either very shy and reserved or else does not enjoy sporting activities.

HOUSE-SWAPPING

This is probably the best way to get good-quality accommodation for a reasonable price. Self-catering in properties exclusively rented out often means poor equipment and drab or institutional-looking furniture, whereas swapping your own house with someone else's family home means that you will almost certainly meet the same standards of comfort that you leave behind – sometimes higher. If you are interested in house-swapping you must register with a company that specializes in this type of holiday (see Useful Addresses, page 62). They will then send you details of the other properties on their books, which are in a number of different countries and locations. For more details you can write to the owners direct, enclosing photographs and information about your own home. It is usually advisable to write a few times so that you can get to know each other and something about each other's lives before you swap. It helps if you have children of roughly the same age, so that the equipment you may need (e.g. cots) and the toys are suitable for the age-group.

Advantages for adults
You have someone to look after your own home – including your garden, animals and house plants – knowing that the 'tenants' will be treating your property with the careful respect with which they hope you will treat theirs. You have the advantages of being able to live like a 'real' native in a comfortable family house, usually with the use of a car, and this will give you an immediate insight into what it is like to live in a foreign country.

Advantages for children
If you swap with a family that also has children, they will enjoy being surrounded by a new set of toys, play equipment and books. There will probably be neighbours or friends that the host family have put you in touch with who may make playmates for your children.

Drawbacks for adults
This type of holiday requires a lot of initial preparation and thought. The best swaps involve leaving copious notes about the idiosyncrasies of your own house and lifestyle (how the petrol gauge never registers empty, what to do when the television goes funny, the best local shop for cheese, the worst time to visit the supermarket). It is considerate to leave the fridge and larder stocked with the basic necessities for the first meal and breakfast, and to arrange that neighbours will offer additional information and help to your guests. You will need to spend time clearing space in cupboards and drawers.

Drawbacks for children
They must treat the other child's possessions with extra respect, and yet must be prepared to find their own interfered with at the end of the holiday. In a country with a different language it may be harder for your children to make friends.

WHAT KIND OF HOLIDAY? 15

ACTIVITY HOLIDAY

The range of these holidays is enormous, and they are to be found both at home and abroad (see Useful Addresses, page 62). In essence, the holiday is built around a particular sport or activity, such as skiing, sailing, tennis, pony-trekking or cycling. Although some activity holiday specialists make provision for the younger members of the family, they are usually unsuitable for babies and young children. But over the age of about seven, if the child shares the family enthusiasm for a particular pursuit, like sailing, it can work very well, giving you a unique opportunity to play and learn together. Even better from the point of view of many families are the holidays that offer a number of different activities, so that each member of the family can take up a different hobby, or change half-way through. Accommodation and food are often of a lower standard than the purely relaxing holidays.

Skiing holidays are usually somewhat different, in that they may not be aimed specially at families, as in other activity packages. You will have to check what the tuition and baby-sitting facilities are.

Advantages for adults
It is a good opportunity to gain or refine a skill without excluding the children, and to develop an interest in common with them, which adds to your relationship.

Advantages for children
Older children enjoy the learning and improvement involved, and find it good to share a strong interest with their parents.

Drawbacks for adults
The holiday will not be a rest, as such. Your children might seem keen, in principle, but if they find they *don't* like the chosen activity it can be miserable for everyone. It would be worth checking this out before you book the holiday.

Drawbacks for children
If they don't like the activity or range of activities offered, it is rarely possible to opt out.

PLANNING

Having a good holiday begins well before you leave – in fact months before, when you start to consider the possibilities, make a booking and plan the details. It pays to be thorough at this stage and to think through the potential problems that may arise. You cannot guarantee a trouble-free holiday, but you *can* ensure that you have done your best to avoid problems, and to cover all eventualities.

Booking early is a golden rule, particularly if the holiday you want is much sought after or if you can only go in the peak season. If you all really enjoyed this year's trip and don't yearn for a change, then it can be a good idea to book the same holiday again as soon as the brochures appear – or even on your return. There are sometimes discounts offered for early bookings.

At an early stage you may also be thinking about whether you want to go on holiday with another family. This is usually worth considering if you are going on a self-catering holiday in Britain or abroad, where your chosen accommodation is relatively isolated and there are unlikely to be play or care facilities for children. The company of another family means that you can share childcare and your children have others to play with. But do remember, this *can* put a strain on the relationship between the adult couples and even on the friendships between the children, so you have to make your choice of friends quite carefully. It is also important that you have enough space to get away from each other – to relax or grumble – or, even better, to have adjacent but separate living accommodation.

If your children are very small, and company for them is not an issue, then you may need to think about supervision. Crawlers and toddlers need to be watched every minute of the time they are awake and your holiday setting may not be as child-proof as your own home. Even fairly sensible primary-school-age children can get themselves into uncharacteristic trouble in an unfamiliar environment if they encounter new dangers which they do not recognize.

When your children are older and do not need to be watched constantly, finding the right company for them becomes very important, particularly if they do not have a sibling close enough in age to be much of a companion. But in fact most siblings will enjoy each other's company on holiday more than they do at home. If you have only one child and you have chosen a holiday that does not provide plenty of potential companions, it can sometimes work out well if your child invites a friend to come along too.

Your other main consideration will be when to go on holiday. Until you have school-age children it is best to avoid school holidays if possible. Peak-season holidays are the most expensive, and there are fewer interesting discounts. The holiday resorts are more crowded, and abroad it is often too hot for most children. Remember that, even when your children are of school age, you can choose the Easter or Christmas holidays for your break, or even half-terms. If the school gives a week off for half-term, that gives you ten days of holiday time if you leave on the Friday afternoon and come back late on Sunday. Legally children can miss up to two weeks of school for your family holiday. You may not want to make use of this, especially if your child is older, but a few days tacked on to half-term will give you a reasonable period off-season.

Planning is the key to good organization and a successful holiday. Below we highlight the main points to consider and check out before you go.

PLANNING 17

YOUR DESTINATION

Once you have decided on the category of holiday you want to take, you must narrow down the specific area you wish to go to, taking into account the ages and inclinations of your children. If you want to go on a package holiday, then you will need to get hold of a range of brochures to choose the exact location. If you have decided on self-catering in Britain, you will be choosing between the country, seaside or town. In the same way, you may be looking into the position of camp-sites and the facilities they have to offer.

Before finally making up your mind, you will want to find out everything you can about the place that you have chosen. First and foremost you wish to know what facilities it offers, but you also need to know all about its shortcomings – so that you can change your mind, or pack and compensate accordingly.

READING THE SMALL PRINT

First, shop around for the best deal. The prices – even for identical rooms in the same hotel – can vary by quite a bit between companies, and many holiday operators have special offers for children. It is certainly worth ploughing through the brochures and adding up exactly what each one is offering you, and deciding whether the 'free' holiday for your baby is actually subsidized by the fact that you have to pay a high price for the hired cot. If you have the time it is also worth seeing whether you can cut costs further by avoiding travel companies altogether. 'Package holidays' do not always represent the best deal. You are paying for the services of a courier at your destination, and for the convenience of having the whole holiday arranged for you. Dealing direct with the owners of a self-catering apartment, or choosing a small hotel and making your own reservation as well as booking your own flight often saves you money.

If you have chosen your holiday from a brochure it is most important to examine the details carefully. Holiday companies are bound by strict laws, and they are not allowed to misrepresent the holidays they are selling. But on the other hand they do not have to highlight what they *do not* offer. For instance, if you find yourself on the third floor of an apartment building having to carry all your baby gear up and down stairs two or three times a day, it is no good complaining *unless* the

brochure said the hotel had lifts. So try to think about what the brochure may be leaving out when you read what is on offer.

Also remember that brochure writers tend to have a vocabulary all their own. Be alert for certain imprecise words that may have a hidden meaning. 'Lively', for instance, usually means 'noisy'. 'Friendly' is no guarantee that the management will treat you like their own family, but can be an indication that the hotel is small and without many facilities for the brochure to sell. 'Quiet', for a holiday cottage, is likely to mean isolated. Brochure reading requires a certain amount of cynicism and common sense if you are to build up a moderately realistic picture of your destination.

When considering booking a self-catering holiday through a brochure or from a small ad in the paper, you will need extra information before making up your mind. You can often ask to see photographs – inside the property as well as out – and have an opportunity to speak to the owner direct about the accommodation and the area. Camp-sites vary too, not only in location, but also in layout and facilities. Two sites quite close together may be very different and you will want to find out what is on offer. Be sure to get pictures of the site, which will give you useful information about how closely packed the tents and caravans are, for instance.

THE HOLIDAY AREA

If you are buying through a travel agent you may be able to coax them into giving you a clearer picture of your chosen hotel and resort. The *Agent's Hotel Gazetteer*, which most travel agents keep in the back room or under the desk, gives a more truthful and less rosy picture of hotels than are described in the brochures. It also includes maps so that you can see where the hotel is in relation to the beach, for instance, and how many roads you may have to cross.

It is obviously in your travel agent's interests to sell you a holiday you will be happy with so that you will return to book again, so do spend the time discussing your needs with him. If he knows the ages and temperaments of your children, as well as the kind of holiday you like, he may come up with a solution that suits you all.

If you are not using a travel agent, get the information you need directly from the person you are dealing with, or from the relevant tourist office. *Which?* magazine has a holiday supplement, and most libraries carry back copies for you to consult.

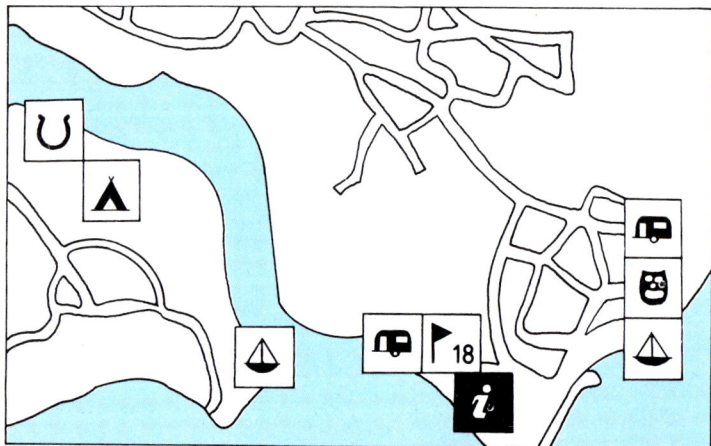

PLANNING 19

Below you will find lists of some of the most generally relevant points to consider or to find out more about. You can adapt these according to the type of holiday you choose, and the ages of your children.

SUGGESTED QUESTIONS

▶ Is it a good place for family holidays, or does it attract mainly the young and unattached or the older traveller whose family has grown up? This is important from the whole family's point of view. Your children will like to make friends, and so will you. Also other parents are more tolerant of children and their foibles. Young singles as well as retired people may be easily irritated by your noisy or merely high-spirited brood.

▶ Is it easy to get around? If you are taking a pushchair, are the roads steep or level, pot-holed or well-maintained? The younger your children the less likely it is that you will want to travel any further once you have reached your destination.

▶ Where does your rented accommodation or hotel stand in relation to other facilities? Is it isolated or central?

▶ Check exactly what is on offer for the different age groups, in the way of sport and entertainment, and find out if the equipment is provided or whether you have to pay extra to hire it.

▶ What are the local shops like? Is there a supermarket close by? Can you buy disposable nappies there and roughly how much do they cost?

▶ If there is any food or medicine that you or your family can't do without, check whether it is available where you are going. If the answer is an honest 'I don't know', you may decide it is safer to pack it anyway.

▶ Can you get the baby food your child likes and what does it cost?

▶ Is the beach sandy? If so, what colour is it? (sometimes it's volcanic and black!). Brochures may neglect to mention that a beach is pebbly – which, although it need not ruin a holiday, is certainly less enjoyable for children than sand. You will also want to know how large the beach is – sometimes a lot of holidaymakers are expected to converge on a very narrow strip.

▶ Are the waters clean and safe? It is important to know whether the sea is safe if you are planning to let your children spend a lot of time in it. The best kind of beach is a wide strip of sand and a long shallow expanse of sea, either gently shelving or only becoming deep some way out.

- Are there any hazards, such as strong tides, jellyfish, or other nasties?
- Are there facilities, such as cafés, and equipment, such as sun umbrellas, on the beach?
- What is there to do if the weather is bad? In a beach resort you will want to know what the rainy-day facilities are, whereas in a skiing resort you would need to know what the contingency plans are for when there is no snow. In the town or country in Britain you will want to know what the other local tourist attractions are.
- If you are taking a 'country cottage', is it in a truly rural location? Are there plenty of public footpaths nearby, and where is the nearest farm?

YOUR ACCOMMODATION

Whether you are staying in a hotel, a rented house or apartment, or even a camp-site, you will need to consider its location and its furniture or equipment very carefully.

- What is its position in relation to the beach, the ski-slopes, good walks, the pool, the shops, the restaurants or the play facilities? You do not want to have to walk too far to the focal point of your holiday.
- How near is it to a busy road?
- Is the position noisy – near, or containing, an all-night disco, for example, or on a main road with heavy traffic going past?
- What baby equipment is provided? Are there highchairs and good-quality cots?

Staying in a hotel

- If it is on a busy road, is it possible to specify quiet rooms at the back?
- What meals are included in the price? Check what breakfast includes: if it is a hearty, serve-yourself meal, then half-board may be entirely adequate, allowing you to get yourself a light snack at midday and freeing you from having to stay near your hotel.
- Do highchairs and cots cost extra, or are they included in the overall price?
- Is there a good secluded play area for little ones? Check exactly what this consists of. Sometimes it is only a bit of brown scrubby grass with a rusty swing. It should be well-protected and shady, with perhaps its own paddling pool and a range of safe climbing equipment.
- Is there a children's club? What ages does it cater for, how often does it meet and what do they do with the children? If you are travelling off-season, you should also check whether the club operates at that time.

- ▶ If there are sports facilities for older children, check exactly what is on offer and whether equipment is provided or you have to pay extra to hire it.
- ▶ Is there a laundry, and what does it charge? Alternatively, is there a nearby launderette?
- ▶ Are there early meals for children? If so can they sometimes eat with you if you prefer? Some hotels offer separate sittings for children, which can be useful for younger ones if you are trying to keep them to roughly the same timetable you have at home. But if they are allowed to stay up with you in the evenings you may prefer to have them with you at table as well.
- ▶ Is there a baby-sitting service? What does it cost, and what does it consist of? Some hotels operate an intercom service, whereby the switchboard operator can listen in to the rooms and alert you if your baby cries. If you are planning to go out, or fear that your child would be upset to wake alone in an unfamiliar room, you may want to arrange for a sitter to stay in the room.
- ▶ Which floor is your bedroom on? If it is higher than first floor and you have an infant or toddler, you will also wish to know if there is a lift. If your children are old enough to work the lift on their own, you will want to know whether it is safe. In some countries there is an age limit below which no child can go in a lift unaccompanied by an adult.
- ▶ Does your bedroom have a balcony? If so you will need to know that it is completely safe for young children, with bars close enough together so that they cannot squeeze through and high enough so that it is hard to climb over.
- ▶ Is there a bath? Some small children do not like showers. This is less of a problem if the shower head detaches and can be brought down to the level of a child, so that the water does not run in her eyes. You can also get round this by sluicing the child down with water in a bucket or a bowl, or by taking a travel bath-plug with you to stop up the plug hole and sit the child in the tray with a couple of inches of water in it.

Renting a cottage or apartment

- ▶ Do you have to put down a deposit in case of breakages and losses? (Remember to check the inventory when you arrive, so that you are not penalized for something that was not there in the first place.)
- ▶ Do you have your own washing machine? What are the facilities for drying clothes? Is there a launderette nearby?

- Are you supposed to bring your own bed linen and towels?
- Is a maid service available for cleaning the house or apartment?
- What kitchen equipment is provided?
- Is it possible to shut off the kitchen from the living space? Kitchens are dangerous areas for toddlers and small children, and these are likely not to be as child-proof as your own.
- Is there a garden, and is it safe?
- Do you have your own television?
- Is there a telephone, and is it metered or coin in the slot?
- How is the house heated, and how do you pay for it?
- Is electricity included in the rental, or will you need coins for slot meters?
- When it says 'sleeps six', what exactly does it mean? (Sometimes this includes the use of a sofa-bed in the sitting room.)
- Who can you contact in case of problems?
- Ask for the name of someone who has stayed there before for reference purposes.

Camp-sites and caravan-sites

- What facilities are on offer (washrooms, laundries, swimming pools, entertainment)?
- What are the site rules?
- What exactly do the caravans or tents consist of and how much space is there?
- Are there proper beds?
- What is provided in the way of kitchen equipment, cutlery and crockery?
- How far apart are the tents/caravans?

BEFORE YOU GO

You will have checked out everything you need to know about your destination at the time of booking, but there are a few other things to consider well before you leave for your holiday.

▶ If it is your first holiday abroad since your child was born, you must remember to have her included on your passport well before you have to travel. You should do this at least six weeks before you are due to set off – though even earlier is better, so that you can avoid the nerve-racking worries that official delays inevitably cause.

It is worth putting the children on both your passports in case for some reason one of you needs to return home early, which could otherwise mean dragging the children away before the end of their holiday.

▶ Check with your doctor in plenty of time about any health precautions you need to take for your destination such as vaccinations (see Health and First Aid, page 53).

▶ Involve your children in the planning as time draws near. Very young ones will not understand much, but older children will like to look at the brochure or other pictures of the country or area you are going to, and will enjoy plotting what they can do and see. If you are going to a foreign country, there are some excellent 'background' books written for older children.

▶ If you are taking your own travel cot, buy or borrow it well in advance, and let your baby sleep in it for a couple of weeks before you leave, so that it will be a familiar haven in unfamiliar surroundings.

▶ Try to accustom your baby to taking a cold bottle, or jars of food, before you go, if she is not used to this. There will be times on holiday when you don't want the bother of heating them up.

▶ Make sure you have the ingredients for an easy meal when you return home, or something in the freezer that you can just heat through. You don't want to have to worry about organizing it on your return, when all of you are likely to be tired.

▶ Take out holiday insurance well ahead of your departure date. Choose a policy that gives adequate medical cover if you are going abroad (see Private Insurance, page 61), and which gives full reimbursement in the event of you having to cancel your holiday whether you are holidaying at home or abroad. However unlikely that seems, the risks of cancellation increase the more children you have, any one of whom could get ill at the last minute.

▶ If you will be hiring a car at your destination, make sure you book one with child safety seats or restraints appropriate to the ages of your children. You may need to take your own rearward-facing child seat or booster seat if only adult seat belts are provided.

▶ If you are going from an airport, work out well in advance how you are going to get there and book a taxi, or ask a neighbour to take you, in plenty of time. Plan to do whatever is least disruptive for yourselves and the children. If you need to, reserve a place in the long-term car park well ahead. You may even need to stay overnight near the airport if you have a very early morning flight.

▶ Make sure you have sufficient money – in foreign currency coins or notes if travelling abroad – to cover any incidental travel expenses such as refreshments for the children if you incur delays, or any unforeseen transport charges.

24 TRAVELLING WITH CHILDREN

WHAT TO TAKE

This chapter looks specifically at the clothes and other items that you are likely to need for your children on holiday, and for a baby in particular. It also considers what extras you should take if you are going on a self-catering holiday. It should be read in conjunction with the following two chapters: Travel Equipment deals with the portable equipment that you should consider taking on holiday, particularly if you have a baby, and All You Need for Your Journey concentrates on essentials that you need for a journey with children, much of which you will also need at your destination.

The golden rule is to take as little as possible – but not to leave behind anything you will really need. This is best achieved by making lists: first a checklist of clothing and underwear for each person travelling, then other lists of linen, towels and equipment that you deem necessary. Once you have listed everything you can think of – weed out: ask yourself whether each item is strictly necessary, or whether you could do without it. It is also useful to have a dummy run: lay out the clothes and equipment, and see how you are going to be able to pack them, and how much the total weighs, if you have a weight limit.

When deciding what to leave behind, you should consider not taking anything that you can hire or buy at your destination, unless the cost would be prohibitive. From the point of view of packing, you should also remember that you may need an extra bag for transporting home anything you do buy while away. A soft squashy bag that can be packed at the bottom of your case is ideal. But again, consider leaving behind any of the cheaper items that you bought for the holiday – and possibly donating them to another family – particularly if they are bulky, such as large buckets, spades or fishing nets. Consider them one of the expenses of the trip, in the same way as snacks and drinks you will buy while there.

Remember to find out whether you *can* buy what you need at your destination before deciding to leave it behind. Check through whoever has handled your booking. If they are not sure, you will have to decide whether to take the risk or pack the items anyway. It is also a good rule to go for disposable rather than permanent items, particularly in the case of nappies and bibs. That way you only need to pack what is necessary for the journey, and then can buy the rest at your destination. It also saves you washing unnecessarily.

WHICH CLOTHES TO PACK?

When deciding on clothes to take for the children, remember that the under-fives are particularly messy. Unless you are prepared to spend a lot of time washing, you should take some extra clothes to cope with this. The amount of clothes you take will also depend on the season, type of holiday, and whether you have access to a washing machine. If the weather is likely to be cool or cold the clothes you take will also be correspondingly more bulky, and will be more difficult to wash and dry. Choosing clothes that you can build up in layers to provide warmth goes some way to compensating for this, and you can wear some of the bulkier items for the journey. If the weather is hot you are likely to spend a lot of the day virtually undressed, and will therefore need fewer items.

The most practical clothes are those that don't crush when packed, and don't need ironing when washed. However, you can avoid ironing

▶ *See page 26 for hot-weather clothes checklist*

even items that usually need it by hanging them out carefully after washing. Easing garments into the correct shape and smoothing out creases while the items are still damp works very well.

THE ART OF PACKING

There is an art to packing. Some people are able to get far more than others into the same size case by skilfully 'nesting' articles. Careful packing also means that you arrive with clothes that are wearable, rather than crushed beyond recognition. It is worth taking your time to do this properly, and working out ways that you can save space.

▶ Stuff underwear and uncrushable baby clothes into shoes, or anything hollow and rigid you might be taking, such as your baby's favourite dish.
▶ Insert books into crevices at the very end.
▶ Lay crushable articles as flat as possible, and if you have to fold them, lay tissue paper over the garment before you do so.
▶ Try only to make horizontal folds, which will fall out once the garment is hung up, particularly if you do this in a steamy bathroom.

▶ Another method of ensuring that you arrive with uncrushed clothes is to make a large sausage of them. Lay the clothes out flat on the bed, one on top of the other, and then form them into a roll. This is particularly appropriate if you have a nylon sausage-shaped bag.

Use lightweight hold-alls or suitcases, particularly if you are going to be carrying them for any length of time. The straps and handles should be wide and comfortable so that they do not cut into you while you are carrying them. A lightweight sausage-shaped bag, packed only with soft clothes and no hard items, can also double as a bolster for sleeping children on the journey. Rucksacks are particularly useful because you can carry them on your back with the minimum of strain; children can also be issued with small-sized ones.

Bags with integral wheels are a boon if you are travelling by train or plane, as you will be able to roll them along the ground. You can buy sets of wheels attached to a trolley to place any bag or case on, and this is worth considering if your bag does not have its own wheels.

HOLIDAY CHECKLIST: ESSENTIALS FOR A BABY

Wherever your final destination, and whatever type of holiday you choose, if you have a young child there are certain items you will have to find room for.

▶ Any favourite toy or comforter that your baby or child needs to help him settle down for the night.
▶ Your child's favourite cup or dish, if he is reluctant to eat or drink from anything else.
▶ Safety harness and, if appropriate, walking reins.
▶ Extras for making your accommodation safe and child-proof (see Safety on Holiday, page 49): masking tape, string and table corner protectors.
▶ Anything specific to your child's health or special needs, such as a spare pair of spectacles for a child who wears them or an inhaler for an asthmatic child.
▶ Extra protection in the form of highest-factor sun cream etc.

▶ *See pages 28–30 for travel equipment*

Bottle-feeding
You will need to take your whole sterilizing kit with you if your baby is under six months old. Take your baby's own brand of powdered milk formula, if you have discovered that you cannot buy it at your holiday destination.

Nappies
Most places you are likely to travel to will sell disposable nappies, so you only need enough for the journey. The extra expense of buying them at your destination is outweighed by the convenience of not having to pack and carry them.

For some older babies disposables are inadequate to deal with night-time wetting. You may want to pack a couple of terry nappies to use only at night. You can work on the 'one on, one in the wash' principle, sterilizing and rinsing the used nappy through in the morning. In this case you may need to take some nappy sterilizing powder as well as some nappy liners.

Food
If your baby is a fussy eater and will only eat a particular brand of food which you may not be able to obtain at your destination, you will probably have to take your own. It is more convenient, as well as lighter in weight, if this can be bought in packet form, rather than jars or tins.

HOLIDAY CHECKLIST: HOT WEATHER

Clothes
You need the minimum of clothes for a hot climate, particularly if you are going on a beach holiday. Your children will live in swimming togs and light cover-ups most of the time. Clothes rinsed through in the evening will usually be dry and ready to wear by morning, so you need not even duplicate too many outfits if you are prepared to do a little washing.

▶ Choose clothes made of a light cotton material. Be sure to include some with long sleeves and legs if your children are fair and have delicate skin, or in case they get sunburnt and need to cover up.
▶ Sun hats are essential if it is very hot, and should preferably be worn all the time.
▶ Plastic beach shoes are good for use when the ground is very hot and for paddling in rocky waters. These can probably be bought quite cheaply at your destination if you want to save room in your travelling bags.
▶ At least one warm outfit per child, in case the weather turns unexpectedly cold.
▶ A light waterproof jacket for the days when it rains.
▶ You may need one or two presentable outfits if your child will be eating with you in the hotel.

Other essentials
▶ A flask for days on the beach. Take the unbreakable variety that come in children's lunchboxes.
▶ Sun cream and aftersun preparations (see Health and First Aid, page 53) – but you may prefer to buy them at your holiday destination, provided they are not too expensive.
▶ Insect-repellent cream or gel to deter mosquitoes from biting you and your children. You will need an antihistamine cream too, to alleviate itching from the odd mosquito bite.
▶ Arm-bands or rubber rings for swimming.
▶ Bucket and spade and an inflatable beach ball. You can buy these when you arrive if space is more important than money.
▶ An insect net to drape over the baby's cot.

▶ *See page 24 for which clothes to pack*

HOLIDAY CHECKLIST: COUNTRY AND COLD WEATHER

In cold climates, the insides of hotels, apartments and houses will usually be well heated, and often exceptionally warm.

▶ Take mainly lightweight clothes, which you can wear when inside. Worn in layers for when you go outside, they provide plenty of warmth because thin layers trap pockets of warm air between them and so insulate your body.
▶ Woolly hat, possibly with ear muffs if you are skiing.
▶ Good gloves.
▶ Warm, waterproof outerwear. Anoraks or padded coats with a waterproof covering are better all-purpose, all-weather wear than other types of coat.
▶ Walking shoes.
▶ Wellington boots.
▶ Proper boots if you are going skiing. You can buy these before you go, but they will take up a lot of space in your baggage. It is a good idea to find out whether you can hire the appropriate warm-lined boots at the resort.

SELF-CATERING CHECKLIST

▶ Your own bed linen. You will have checked whether this is provided at your destination.
▶ Plastic undersheet for babies, and also young children who are not reliably dry at night.
▶ Towels. Take plenty if there is no washing machine.
▶ Tea towels.
▶ A good kitchen knife will save you irritation if the only one on offer is blunt.
▶ Bottle- and tin-openers and any other convenient kitchen gadgets you would miss.
▶ Loo paper. Take at least one roll for when you arrive, until you can get to the shops.
▶ A portable clothes line and a supply of pegs.
▶ Washing soap for clothes. If hot water is going to be hard to obtain, choose a biological detergent that cleans through soaking in cold or lukewarm water.
▶ Dry-cleaning fluid. Take one that claims to remove tar-stains, which are all too easily picked up at the beach.
▶ A travel iron and an adaptor plug if travelling abroad.
▶ Food for the first day, particularly if you will be arriving at night or late on a Saturday.
▶ Favourite foods that would be hard to obtain and that your children would miss.
▶ Torch in the event of a power cut and to help you see your way outdoors at night.
▶ Mending kit, containing spare buttons, small scissors, poppers, velcro and elastic, needles and thread.

TRAVEL EQUIPMENT

In acknowledgement of the fact that more and more parents are travelling with children – and very young ones at that – it is now possible to buy a complete range of foldaway lightweight equipment and disposable items that can make life away from home very much easier. Thankfully, the older your children become the less special equipment they need, but the smaller ones seem to need an inordinate amount of paraphernalia in relation to their size! Of course, it would be impracticable to think about taking every item available – even if you were able and willing to buy them, carrying it all would still pose a problem in anything but a small truck.

The following is a survey of what travel equipment is on offer for the very young; most of the items are readily available from good stores. They are not all *essential*. You will have to work out which items you would find most useful at the other end, and to look at your available baggage weight or space allowance to see if you have the capacity to take them. If an item is *not* going to be constantly in use, or it won't make your life appreciably easier on your holiday, you are going to resent carrying it even more on the journey back.

SAFETY HARNESS
This should be used for added security when your child is in the pushchair or highchair, as well as with a rein for walking.

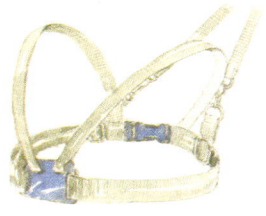

PUSHCHAIR
This is one of the most essential items, and it is worth sacrificing something else to squeeze it in. The freedom it gives you both while you are travelling and when you reach your destination makes it worth its weight in gold. It *does* take up space, even when folded, but its weight is not a problem as it is usually being wheeled. The best pushchairs for travelling are lightweight, compact and easily collapsible; if yours is a heavier, more bulky model you may want to consider buying or borrowing a lightweight one in time for the holiday. The seat should preferably be adjustable so that the baby can either sit or lie back to sleep while you are walking or waiting about at the airport or on a ferry or train. It is also useful to take a clip-on parasol or canopy to shield your baby from the sun, as well as the waterproof hood and apron, as rain is a possibility wherever you are.

BABY CARRIER
This is useful for younger babies especially if they have been used to being carried in this way. A backpack can also be a bonus for heavier babies, particularly when you are travelling without a car and need to have your hands free for the rest of your luggage or older children.

CHANGING BAG
These soft, lightweight bags with spongeable interiors have useful pockets for nappies and toiletries. Some unzip to provide a changing surface; others have a separate changing mat, which may be more convenient. Some bags have a separate zipped compartment to hold a potty or soiled nappies.

TRAVEL COT
This is essential if a cot is not provided at your destination, unless you can hire one there. Try to accustom your baby to it well before you go. Travel cots fold flat to make storage and carrying easier.

NIGHT-LIGHT
If your child is frightened of the dark, or not used to it, then it makes sense to take a night-light on holiday with you. The sort that plug directly into the socket are the most compact, but you will have to take an adaptor plug if you are travelling abroad.

POTTY
This is essential if your child is only recently out of nappies. It is possible to buy a travel potty with a lid which keeps the contents from spilling until you can empty it. Another useful option is an inflatable potty, which you use with disposable liners. A toilet training seat, which fits over the adult loo seat, is very much an optional extra, *unless* your toddler has been using it consistently and would be unhappy without it.

BABY BATH
This is not essential and is something of a space-waster, unless you pack it tightly with other things. It is usually possible to improvise a baby bath for the time you are on holiday. A washing-up bowl will suffice for a small baby, or even the sink, provided you lay a large flannel or small towel on the bottom to protect the baby from the plug and cover the hot tap with a towel so that the baby does not burn himself. It might be worth taking a rubber non-slip mat for the bottom of the bath.

HIGHCHAIR

Most highchairs fold down to a more packable shape, but are a luxury item if space is at a premium. Unless you have a lightweight, folding highchair you may think of other alternatives for your holiday. A removable rearward-facing car seat can double as a baby's chair as, of course, does the pushchair. For feeding, you can use a clip-on tray that will fit most pushchairs and strollers, as well as the car seat.

Another alternative is to pack a small-sized chair with its own tray; some models can eventually be converted into a highchair with the addition of a matching stand. For small babies, a foldaway table seat is very light and compact and clips easily on to a stable surface, most usually a table. With toddlers, who prefer to sit on an adult chair, it is only height that is a problem. You could take a booster block or seat with you, which straps on to the adult seat and raises a child to adult height. By turning it around you have the choice of two different heights.

BIB

Cloth bibs mean extra washing while on holiday but disposable bibs are now readily available and are much better for travelling. Otherwise take a rigid plastic bib with a pocket to catch spills; it only needs to be rinsed and wiped clean after use.

TRAINER MUG

These are useful for travelling even after your children have grown out of them. Most of them twist to seal, or have additional sealer lids, so that they are useful for carrying drinks, and the spout makes for spill-proof drinking on a bumpy journey.

FOOD HEATER

It is possible to buy a small, portable food heater to warm bottles and jars, but they are really only necessary if your baby is a fussy eater who refuses food that is not at the preferred temperature. Baby food does not have to be warmed, and neither do bottles. It does the baby no harm to eat or drink them cold, and it is a good idea to get him used to this before you go on holiday.

The foldaway table seat is an ideal travel substitute for a highchair. It is lightweight and folds flat in your luggage and can be clipped on to any sturdy table.

ALL YOU NEED FOR YOUR JOURNEY

The journey is an important part of your holiday, and for it to pass pleasantly you have to be well-equipped and prepared. It makes sense to have a bag or two packed only with the things you need for the journey itself so that you do not have to rummage through the rest of your luggage to find what you want. This chapter lists the main requirements that will ensure the smoothest of journeys and have you prepared for every eventuality. But if you are travelling alone with the children or are very restricted as to the amount of baggage you can take, you may find it all too much to carry. If this is the case, use your common sense and weed the items down further – at the end of the chapter we pare the list down to the bare essentials, according to the mode of transport you have chosen. As a rule of thumb, the younger your child the more paraphernalia you need. As your children grow older they need less and are likely to be more helpful too.

CARRYING THE ESSENTIALS

When it comes down to it, what you take is restricted to what you can practically carry, unless you are travelling all the way by car. Being burdened with heavy luggage is tiring and stressful, though if the items you are carrying help to keep your children occupied and sweet-tempered, you are likely to feel it is worth it. Remember that you won't be carrying the entire weight for all the journey – consumable items, like food and drink, go rapidly, leaving your bag lighter.

Choose bags that are easy to carry – either a rucksack style, or bags with wide shoulder straps or wide carrying handles, so that when filled and heavy the straps don't cut into you. Avoid plastic supermarket carrier bags at all costs, even for carrying your food supplies. They can be a disaster as the carrying handles condense

Even quite young children are capable of carrying a lightweight rucksack. Pack it with their own toys and a spare sweater.

▶ *See pages 39–48 for diverting children on a journey*

into thin hard strings that cut off the circulation in your hands – otherwise they break, leaving you to carry the bag in your arms.

Distribute the load as much as possible for easier carrying. It makes sense to have separate bags for different things (unless you are trying to get everything into one): a bag for cleaning equipment, one for food and so on. Enlist as many people as possible to help you carry them. If two adults are making the journey this is quite easy. But even smallish children can carry a bag of their own, particularly of the satchel or rucksack type. This is a good place to put most of the toys and games that will be keeping them occupied during the journey, though it is just as well to have a few spare ones hidden in the event of a long delay. Children can also carry their own sponge bag and nightwear if you are making a stop en route. They will enjoy the independence and responsibility of carrying their own luggage.

CLOTHES

It is useful to carry a spare clean top for each person to change into at the end of the journey. If you are staying overnight on the way, then take a clean set of underwear and perhaps a fresh outfit each. Babies and toddlers will need one or two entire sets of clothes, however short the journey, as it is easy for them to make a mess of themselves. Adults with a young baby should consider taking an extra top for themselves, in case – very likely – the baby leaves sick or posset on their shoulder.

Take a warm top each in case of changes of temperature, and sun hats for the children if you are likely to be outside in the sun for any length of time, such as when queueing for the ferry or waiting around outdoors at a small airport.

If you are making an overnight stop at a hotel, or in a train or ferry cabin, make sure your night things, including wash bag, are separate from the main bulk of your luggage.

CLEAN-UPS

If you are travelling with a baby or toddler still in nappies then you will be fully prepared to take your changing and cleaning kit with you. But even older children and adults need clean-ups on a journey. Travelling is a grubby business, and eating with your hands en route adds to the mess.

▶ A sponge or flannel in a small plastic bag or some commercial wet-wipes. A good alternative is to fold kitchen paper into small squares and spray them with water. These can be stored in a plastic bag and are strong and endlessly useful.

▶ A good supply of plastic bags: either a roll of bin liners, or a stock of supermarket carrier bags smoothed out and folded into squares. These take up very little room and are useful for putting in food rubbish, soiled nappies and dirty clothes. You may also need these on the return journey if you have to pack damp towels or bathing costumes or dirty shoes.

▶ Tissues or a roll of kitchen paper. Kitchen paper is strong enough to mop up spills without disintegrating.

▶ Soap in a tube, rather than a bar, which becomes messy once used.

KIT FOR BABIES

▶ Changing bag with the usual wipes, cream, liners, cotton wool and pins.

▶ A changing surface, such as a fold-up mat or fabric nappy.

▶ Disposable nappies and liners. Take approximately one for every three hours of your journey, and a couple to spare.

▶ Breast pads if breastfeeding.

▶ Potty, preferably with a lid.

▶ Bib, preferably disposable.

▶ Baby's comforter or favourite toy.

FOOD AND DRINK

Aim to take items that do not require utensils or equipment. Snacks should be bite-sized and easily manageable with the fingers (see below). Drinks in cartons with their own straws are good, as they do not spill easily. Cans seem a good idea before they are opened, but younger children can rarely finish them, and unless one is shared between two children, you are likely to have waste, at best, and sticky spillage at worst. It is often better to take a large plastic bottle and some plastic cups so you can dispense small amounts to the thirsty. Have a bottle filled with plain water too. Even children who insist they don't like water will find it thirst-quenching when they are really hot.

Bottle-fed babies
Take enough made-up bottles for the journey, with extra for delays. Keep them cold in a cool bag. Alternatively you can keep boiled water in a sterile thermos flask and mix the feeds as you go. To cut down on carrying bottles you can buy disposable bottle liners and then you only need the one bottle and a couple of spare teats. Baby's milk does not have to be warmed before drinking.

Recently-weaned babies
The baby will probably enjoy the finger foods that you provide for the rest of the family, or his own rusks. Otherwise baby food in jars is the easiest to handle, if bulky to carry. Jars can be heated in a wide-mouthed thermos if you need to do this. Remember to throw away any uneaten food from the jar.

Useful equipment
You should keep eating utensils to the minimum, as you don't want to have to wash anything. Useful standbys are plastic spoons, a drinking cup with a spout, and plastic cups. It is also convenient to have a bottle/can opener and a small sharp knife.

TUCK BOX

One of the best ways of keeping children happy is to have a variety of things for them to eat and drink. These are some ideas:
▶ sandwiches cut into quarters and with the crusts removed
▶ plain sweet biscuits
▶ small cocktail savoury biscuits
▶ individual packs of raisins
▶ cubes of hard cheese
▶ a bag of prepared vegetable sticks – carrot, celery, cucumber, cauliflower florets – which can be eaten on their own or (for older children) dipped into a small carton of plain yoghurt
▶ small eating apples, or peeled and cored apple cubes rubbed with lemon juice and kept in a bag
▶ grapes, preferably seedless
▶ small strips of firm omelette, plain or flavoured with cheese

Avoid:
▶ peanuts – they can cause a child to choke
▶ soft, messy fruits, such as oranges, bananas or strawberries
▶ greasy snacks such as sausages or pastry-covered items, especially if the children are prone to travel sickness

Drinks
▶ fruit juice in small cartons with their own straw
▶ fill large, empty plastic bottles with plain water, very dilute squash or cordial, or fresh fruit juice mixed half and half with water

TOYS AND GAMES

These are *not* luxuries. Keeping your children amused and entertained on the journey is the key to you all having a pleasant time. A bored child is also a handicap and will make any journey seem longer and more arduous.

For a list of useful toys to pack, see Good Toys or Diversions, page 40. Older children can take a few in their own bags – but do not allow them to carry anything valuable such as a personal stereo or a camera unless they are using it at the time. Once occupied with other pastimes there is a chance that they might leave their bags unattended. Dissuade older children from taking anything that is large and cumbersome or heavy, or a toy that would be spoilt if pieces were lost.

For your own sanity, avoid taking any toys with an irritating noise, such as whistles, loud rattles, talking dolls or computer games which bleep. These will drive you mad in a small car, and will alienate other passengers in enclosed spaces, such as trains or coaches.

Anything with too many 'bits' is not a good idea, as these can get lost. If you do take them, you may want to pack duplicates in your luggage: extra dice, another pack of cards, and so on.

Messy playthings should also be avoided. Pencils and crayons are a better choice than felt tips and ballpoint pens that can stain clothes. Plasticine or modelling clay can stick to hair, clothes and upholstery in cars, trains or planes.

EMERGENCIES

For emergencies of any kind, it is important to have your first aid kit handy (see page 60). Even if you don't carry it in your journeying hand luggage, it should be easily accessible in your main luggage or in the car. If your first aid kit is well-equipped and used items are constantly replaced, this is one less thing that you have to worry about at the last moment. Other useful standbys are scissors – the foldaway variety are good – a small sewing kit, plenty of safety pins and a plastic container with a lid for if a child feels sick at a time when you cannot easily stop the car.

Make sure you carry coins for the telephone box, and a list of any emergency numbers you may need, on your person at all times.

▶ *See page 48 for Top Ten Travel Pastimes*

ALL YOU NEED FOR YOUR JOURNEY 35

GETTING ABOUT

Once your children are old enough to walk sensibly on their own and do not need to be carried, moving from place to place is very much easier. But getting about with younger children usually means special equipment of some kind. A pushchair is the best solution for any child who cannot walk, and for a child who tires easily. They can usually go in the hold of an aeroplane and don't need to be taken on as hand luggage. At a pinch a pushchair can be dispensed with in favour of a carrier or sling or a backpack, but you must be prepared for the extra weight to make the journey very tiring for you.

Toddlers and boisterous younger children who are not yet as sensible as you would like usually need some sort of restraint, like a safety harness and walking reins or special hand-held reins for older toddlers. They will save your sanity when you need to give your attention to a smaller child, or to your passport or luggage.

Most of the items listed on the previous pages are essential wherever you are going, however you are travelling and whatever the length of your journey. But the different forms of travel have their own advantages and impose their own restrictions, involving particular considerations, and these are summarized below.

PLANE

You are quite restricted in the amount of hand luggage that you can take on a plane with you. Make sure that the essentials you have to carry are well shared between adults and children.

Absolute essentials
- ▶ Books and quiet toys.
- ▶ Comforters. If your baby likes a dummy or needs a special blanket or toy to help him sleep, you will be sorry if it is in the hold.

Where you can cut down

▶ Except when you have a child in nappies, you will not need to take so much in the way of clean-ups and wipes. Airports and the planes themselves are usually well-equipped in this way; they often carry disposable nappies too.

▶ Although it is always wise to have extra snacks for the children in case they don't like the in-flight meal, you will probably find that the adults are well provided for. Most airlines provide drinks of juice for children on request.

CAR

While it is always important to plan your packing carefully so as to get the maximum in and be sure that you have not left anything essential behind, this is least crucial in a car. Although it is time-wasting and inconvenient, you *can* stop and burrow in the back for another change of clothes, or pull up at a supermarket for extra supplies.

You will not have to worry about how much you take and how heavy it is, or whether it will all fit into a sensible bag. In a car you can stow items in the glove compartment, on the shelves, in the pockets of the seats – and even under the seats, so long as you don't restrict the leg room: this is the one time that ordinary plastic shopping carriers *will* do. It is possible to make stops to jettison rubbish from time to time, or to tuck soiled clothes into the boot.

The children can also travel as comfortably and scruffily as suits you all. In your home-on-wheels they can even wear pyjamas if you are travelling through the night. Messy toddlers and young children can wear old tee-shirts for most of the journey, saving a set of clean clothes for the last leg when you are nearing your destination and may want them to be more presentable.

It is sensible always to keep a first aid kit in the car.

Absolute essentials

▶ Plenty of clean-ups, plastic bags, wipes. If you are going to have to live in your confined space for any length of time, it is important that it is pleasant and non-smelly. If any of your children are likely to be sick, be sure that you have a container or two in case you can't stop in time.

▶ Means of entertainment. With your children so physically restricted it is important that you have packed enough games and toys to keep them involved for most of the time, and that you reserve some of your own energy and good temper for playing games. If you have a baby or toddler in a car seat, a clip-on play and feeding tray is a boon.

Where you can cut down

▶ Snack foods and drinks. You can always pick up extra supplies on the way.

▶ Presentable clothes. It doesn't greatly matter what the children look like, so long as you are able to keep them reasonably clean.

ALL YOU NEED FOR YOUR JOURNEY 37

TRAIN

As with a car, your luggage will be with you as you travel, and although you don't want to have to do so, you can always look through your main luggage for anything you have forgotten to put in your essentials bag.

Absolute essentials

▶ Your clean-up bag. You will be able to rinse dirty hands and face in the train loos, but you may not find anything in the way of soap or towels, and on this most public mode of transport you will want your children to look reasonably presentable.

▶ Change of clothes. For the same reason you may need to be able to put your children into a clean set of clothes if they get dirty.

▶ Enough nappies. You are unlikely to be able to find these in a station shop, and certainly not on the train itself.

Where you can cut down

▶ Snack foods. On any long train journey you should be able to stock up at some point at a buffet or station en route, although you should be sure to take some with you in case the buffet car is closed for any reason. Remember, too, that buying refreshments on the train can work out quite expensive.

COACH

A coach has the same restrictions as a car from the point of view of your children. You lose the advantage of being able to stash your essentials where you like, though you gain in not having to concentrate on the road so that you can give all your attention to the children. It is unlikely that you will be able to get at your main luggage once it is stowed away in the coach.

38 TRAVELLING WITH CHILDREN

Absolute essentials

- ▶ Enough toys and books. For this tedious form of travel it is doubly important to keep the children amused, for their own sakes, and also because of the proximity of other travellers. You can soothe the non-readers by reading to them.
- ▶ Extra clothes. To make sure that you can take advantage of every stop, your children should be able to dress up warmly, and be quite waterproof, so that they can go outside whatever the weather.
- ▶ Your clean-up bag. Stops at service stations will allow you to give your children a thorough clean, but you need to be able to wipe sticky fingers and faces while you are in motion too.

FERRY

If you have driven to the ferry, your travelling essentials may be haphazardly packed in the car. You will be leaving the bulk of your luggage behind, so before you leave the car you should be sure that you have a smaller bag packed with things you will need for the trip itself, as you cannot usually return to the car deck during the journey. The same applies if you have arrived by coach: you need to take with you anything that you will want during the crossing.

Absolute essentials

- ▶ Your night bag, with pyjamas and wash kit, if you have booked a cabin.
- ▶ Enough nappies. You may well not be able to buy these on board.
- ▶ Coats or jackets: it can be cold on deck.

Where you can cut down

- ▶ Snack foods. You do not need to take extras, as you should be able to buy everything you need on board.
- ▶ Toys and games. If you have booked a night crossing and the children will be asleep for most of the time, take the bare minimum to keep them amused while you are waiting to disembark.

ON THE MOVE

Travelling to and from your destination is almost certainly the hardest part of your holiday. On the way out you have the advantage of being excited and keen to get there and for your holiday to begin. On the way back there may be a sense of sadness and anti-climax. On top of that, travelling is quite gruelling, even if it only lasts for a few hours. Most children find it particularly hard to be sitting still, waiting around and expected to be on their best behaviour. Young children have no real concept of time, and you may have to put up with being asked 'Are we nearly there?' every five minutes. That said, you can do a lot to make your journeys easier and to see that they pass as pleasantly as possible for everyone involved.

This section looks at the main forms of transport you are likely to choose and ways of coping with them so that you arrive at least moderately refreshed and not too harassed.

RULES FOR TROUBLE-FREE JOURNEYS

There are a few golden rules that apply generally to all forms of transport. The first, and probably the most important, is to give yourself plenty of time. Remember how difficult, and how wearing, it is to be hurrying the children along all the time and watching the clock every few minutes. Whether you are driving yourself, or have to catch another means of transport at a particular hour, you should aim to avoid rush. Always try to leave more time even than common sense tells you it will take, so as to guard against unforeseeable delays. If you get yourself into a state about timing, this will communicate itself to your children, who will become tense and fretful too. There is no worse start to a holiday than the parents in thundering bad moods and the children tearful or truculent. Of course leaving yourself more time than is strictly necessary can lead to the twin evil of waiting around, and the resulting boredom. However, if you are well provided with diversions and games you will be equipped to deal with this in a positive way and even to appreciate the break it provides.

The next most important point is to dress comfortably. Loose leisurewear, such as cotton tracksuits, is the best choice for all the family. Wear a thin layer underneath, such as a vest or tee-shirt, and have an extra jumper or anorak in a light material. Travelling tends to be a hot business, but there are times when you will be cold too, and wearing layers is the best way of coping with changes in temperature. Comfortable shoes and socks are also important. Anything tight in the way of clothes or footwear will chafe or pinch, and will make sitting or standing for long periods uncomfortable. Children who are at an age to have strong opinions about what they are wearing may fight you on this, but a tight pair of jeans, or a favourite new pair of shoes will seem far less attractive after a few hours of discomfort in them. Remind them that they may prefer to have their favourite clothes clean and ready to wear once they arrive.

The last rule for trouble-free journeys is to be well provided with snacks, changes of clothes, washing kit, toys or games (see All You Need for Your Journey, page 31). If the journey does take longer than you had planned you will all be feeling let down, but if on top of that you are tired and grubby, with nothing to eat or drink, having exhausted all the diversions that you brought along, things will be that much worse! It is worth the inconvenience of carrying heavier hand luggage if it means that you are well provided for.

TRAVELLING BY AIR

Air travel can be divided into the time you spend at the airport, and the hours you spend in the air. Like other forms of travel it also requires some forethought at the booking stage. If you are taking a package holiday you may have little choice about when you depart, but if you do, there are points to consider. Night flights are the least desirable as far as children of any age are concerned. It is impossible for them to snatch more than a few minutes' sleep and the constant awakening and moving from place to place will make them tired and irritable. The timing of return trips should also be looked into. Most hotels and apartments require you to vacate your room before midday, so it is obviously best to have a return flight that fits in with this, or you will have a miserable few hours with your bags packed and your children dressed to go home, unable to do more than wait.

Bear in mind that under-twos are usually not allocated a seat and will have to sit on your lap. Neither do they have a baggage allowance, despite the fact that their equipment is often the most comprehensive and heavy! However you are usually allowed to take a carrycot and pushchair with you without it being included in your own baggage allowance. For both these reasons it is best to try to get a seat by the bulkhead, which gives you more leg-room, and more space to store your belongings – it also means that your lively child's kicking will not disturb the passenger in front! Many airlines let families with young children board early, so this is also worth doing if you want to secure a good place. If you want to breast-feed on the plane, a window seat gives you more privacy.

To make sure that you derive the advantages of the better treatment that travelling with a young baby brings, make it clear when you are booking that you will be travelling with an infant. Some airlines provide a crib or 'skycot' for small babies, so check this, and if they do, it is worth ordering one.

GOOD TOYS OR DIVERSIONS

For babies
▶ a selection of teethers and mobiles
▶ cloth books
▶ building beakers (easy to pack and good for playing in the sand)
▶ a quiet toy with moving parts that requires some manual dexterity, if your baby is at this stage

For older children
▶ packs of cards
▶ dominoes and picture dominoes
▶ magnetic or portable travel games, such as Scrabble, draughts, chess, Connect 4
▶ thick blocks of paper with crayons and pencils
▶ fill-in puzzle or quiz books
▶ picture books
▶ wipe-clean magic slate (also good for scoring games)
▶ magic pictures that appear when rubbed with a pencil
▶ hand or finger puppets
▶ scrapbook and glue in a pen
▶ personal stereo

WAITING TO DEPART

Airports are usually pleasant places to wait, so arriving extra early, as you should, will cause you little hardship. Queueing for ticket and baggage control can be just about the worst part of flying, but if you are one of the first there, you will be at the front of the queue. If the seats have not been allocated already this also allows you to stake your claim for the seats that you want. Remember to ask if families can board early as you do so. Once you have checked in you should go through to the lounge, where you can find a comfortable corner and are close to bar and shops, or where older children can watch the planes. Some departure lounges have a supervised play area for younger children. However, some of the smaller airports may not have café or play facilities in the departure lounge. Remember to check what is on offer before you pass through to the lounge, as you will then be unable to return to the main body of the airport.

All but the smallest airports have good facilities for mothers and babies, where you can feed and change the baby in comfort, ready for the flight. If there is a long delay you can amuse the children with the toys you have brought along, but remember to keep some back for the flight itself. Guard against your baby and children being hungry during delays by packing an extra bottle and snacks.

When boarding time is near, make sure younger children have been to the loo, as it will be a while before they can use the one on the plane. If you are allowed to board first, make sure you do so. Most airlines will allow you to wheel your pushchair to the departure gate itself; it will then be taken and stored in the hold until you arrive.

⬅ TRANSITS ⬅ DEPARTURES ARRIVALS ➡

ON THE PLANE

Because of pressure changes at take-off and landing, your children's ears are likely to block and may feel painful. Sucking and swallowing help release the pressure in the ears, so it is a good idea to give your baby the breast or the bottle at these times. Some food, drinks with a straw or sweets will help older children cope. Yawning is another method for equalizing the pressure in the ears, and you could encourage your child to do so by yawning yourself.

Some airlines, if warned in advance, will provide food for your baby, but it is probably safest to bring your own. Jars are more convenient than tins as they do not need an opener. If the crew are not too rushed they may warm the baby's bottles and the jars of food for you. If you are holding the baby on your lap, let your food and drink cool before you eat it, or turbulence could cause you to spill it and hurt the child.

Children will find the experience of take-off and the bustle of the beginning of the flight exciting, but once you are airborne they are soon likely to feel cooped up and frustrated. Have a few toys and books ready for this eventuality, and bring them out one at a time. Some airlines have a children's pack with drawing materials, perhaps a badge and a simple toy. Ask the air hostess. Older children could do crosswords or quizzes.

It is also worth having your own snack food with you on the flight in case your child is hungry before the in-flight meal is served, or in case he does not like what is on offer. But most children will appreciate the ingredients of the packed meal even if they don't particularly like the taste. They will enjoy keeping the salt and pepper packets as souvenirs of their journey.

TRAVELLING BY CAR

The main advantage that car travel has over every other form of transport is its versatility. The fact that you can start and stop when you want to and go at the pace that best suits you means that you are able to counteract its main drawback – that it is cramped and extremely restrictive for everyone, and particularly hard on active or restive children.

If you have a long journey and timing is absolutely up to you, most seasoned drivers with small children recommend that you do the bulk of the motoring in the late evening and at night. This way you can settle the children to sleep in the back, which takes some of the strain off both the driver and the parent who must keep them amused. You can cover the children with light blankets, or your own coats, and improvise pillows by rolling up their own anoraks. They must, of course, still be secured in their car seats or on booster seats with an adult seat belt.

Of course, for night driving to be successful, there should be two of you to share the driving, so that one of you can catch up on some sleep while the other drives. If you can't get the rest you need to remain alert and vigilant while driving then this is not a good option.

If you have to undertake a very long journey, either in Britain or Europe, you might consider putting your car on the train for at least part of it. As this is overnight you can have a sleeping compartment and all wake refreshed for the final stage of your journey the next morning. Motorail journeys usually have to be booked in advance; though they are expensive they save you the necessity of overnight stops and the cost of petrol.

If you choose to drive during the day, do remember the rule about taking your time. Don't be set on getting there as fast as you can, but aim to be flexible and enjoy the journey. Making frequent stops at beauty spots or places of interest can add an extra dimension to the holiday, and keep the children in a co-operative mood.

When loading the car, pack all you need for your holiday, but try to keep the interior of the car as uncluttered as possible. It is best just to keep the inside of the car for the things that you will need for the journey. If you restrict the children's leg-room with baggage it will make the journey more difficult for all of you as the children will feel uncomfortable sooner.

BABIES

A young baby will almost certainly enjoy the journey. It is well known by parents that the motion of the car soothes most babies to sleep. The views from the window will also be enough to amuse an infant for long periods of time. A bag of toys such as rattles (quiet ones) and teethers can be kept in the front and passed to the baby one by one. Take each toy back once its interest value has dropped, and reintroduce it after a few hours. Attach a clip-on play tray to the baby's car seat if you have one.

Remember to have a light blanket to put over the baby when he drops off to sleep. If you have the windows open at the front the baby will bear the brunt of the draught and can become quite chilled even on a warm day. As with older children, a baby will enjoy tapes of music, either soothing classical music or nursery rhyme tapes that you can sing along to. Even if your baby is still largely breast- or bottle-fed, it is a good idea to offer other drinks, such as plain water or diluted juice, frequently. A baby who is on solids will enjoy some of the finger foods mentioned in Tuck Box, page 33.

With a young baby it is as well to keep to motorways, because the service stations are invaluable as places to rest, feed and change. Most of them now have good mother and baby facilities so that you can breast-feed or change your baby in comfort. With a changing bag (see Travel Equipment, page 29) you can of course also change the baby on the back seat with the car door open.

TODDLERS

The older baby who has started to enjoy the pleasures of moving around will be least happy on a long car ride. A toddler may become quite passionate with anger about having to sit still and be good. You will have to plan a lot of diversionary games and make frequent stops. As a general rule, a short stop for about five minutes every hour is a good minimum to aim for; it gives the children time to run about, use the potty or generally let off steam. Changing where your children sit from time to time will help as well.

Toddlers are at a messy age, and you can guarantee that however much you try, your children will end up dirty. Put them in the clothes you care least about, and keep plenty of spare clothes at hand. If you want them to arrive looking nice, then make the last change of clothes the best one. Remember that one way of keeping down the mess is to use a clip-on feeding tray and make sure that snacks are of the cleanest sort – nothing squelchy or chocolate – and keep the portions small: bite-sized is best. In the same way, give small quantities of drink in a trainer beaker. If you give too much, there may be accidents – the last thing you want is a cross toddler throwing sticky orange juice over the car.

Have a constant stock of small toys to keep your toddler amused. Pass them over one at a time and ask for each one back before you hand over the next. Try to keep some toys back until the end of your journey is in sight. It's a mistake to have used up all the entertainment when there are still hours of driving left. Look at the list of games suggested on page 48. Some of these are suitable, in a modified form, for this age-group too.

If your child has a tantrum or starts to behave particularly badly, you must pull over as this is dangerous. This is the moment for a longer stop, taking enough time to defuse the situation and to calm the toddler down. Explain that the more often this happens the longer the journey will take. If you decide that only a cuddle will calm your excited baby down, you must never bring her on to the front seat, as this is both illegal and highly dangerous. Stop and go into the back yourself so that you can comfort her and play with her while she remains safely strapped in her seat.

OLDER CHILDREN

In some ways older children, with more practice at sitting still, will be the easiest to cope with. Boredom is the main problem, and you will have to keep up a constant stream of diversionary games and story tapes. They will appreciate the stops not only as a chance to stretch their legs, but as interesting changes in their own right. It is worth making small diversions so that you can stop at places of interest even if it makes your journey longer: consult your road map to check on nearby castles or caves.

Arguments are another source of trouble, particularly once children have learnt to say 'It's not fair!'. Personal stereos, though expensive, go some way to helping when children are at loggerheads with each other. You will probably also have to be scrupulous about stopping and letting them shift seats so that everyone has a turn in a favoured position. Obviously you must have properly enforced rules about loud arguments and fighting – both must be banned. The best way of dealing with this is to pull over until everyone has calmed down. Once the children get the message that behaviour like this endlessly delays the journey they will be more motivated to improve.

TRAVELLING BY TRAIN

Travelling by train is one of the better choices with young children. Travel sickness is rare – which is an important consideration for weary parents who have had to clean and change their children once too often. One of the great advantages from the point of view of older children is that they are not confined to a seat. They can walk up and down the compartment, and can even explore the whole train with a willing adult. A sociable child may even make friends with other children or adults. Babies and children of all ages also appreciate the fact that there is plenty to see from the windows when the train is moving and at the stations – even going through a tunnel is exciting. The other bonus is that there is a loo on board. Changing a baby may be a bit of a problem, though more trains now include a changing surface in the cubicle. Although there is almost always running water in the loos, it is usually advisable to take your own supply of soap, towel, flannel and loo paper for clean-ups.

To make your journey as problem-free as possible, it is best to travel at off-peak times when the train is less likely to be crowded – mid-week is usually best, and may even be cheaper. In a less crowded train, people will be tolerant of children's noise because they know they have the option of moving away. Even if you do choose an off-peak train it is wise to reserve seats at the time of booking, and essential to do so if you are travelling at a popular time. It is an idea to ask for the seats to be reserved for you near the restaurant car so that bottles and baby food can be heated up and so that you don't have too far to trek when you need a snack. But you should also bear in mind that restaurant cars may be closed, even when they are advertised as open, so be sure that you have an emergency supply of food and drink to keep the children happy, as well as the usual games and toys to keep them amused.

▶ *See page 48 for Top Ten Travel Pastimes*

TRAVELLING BY COACH

Travelling by coach is the least suitable option if you have young children. Indeed some companies refuse to take babies and it is common for them to stipulate that children must be over twelve before a reservation is accepted for them.

One of the problems of going by coach is that it has all the drawbacks of a car, but – unlike when you are driving yourself – you have little control over when it makes its stops. Children find a coach cramped and restrictive, they cannot move around as they are allowed to on a train, and the scheduled stops are likely to be much further apart than they would like. Sufferers from travel sickness are particularly badly affected as the view of the far horizon is restricted

COPING WITH TRAVEL SICKNESS

If one of your children suffers from travel sickness it can be a misery for you all. Most travel sickness has a purely physical cause: the body is telling the brain that you are sitting still and not moving, while the eye is giving quite different information. Excitement and tension also add to the problem. However there is quite a lot you can do to help.

Prevention
▶ Feed the child at least an hour before you set off – make the meal light, with no rich or greasy food. (Any meals en route should also be light and non-greasy.)
▶ Keep a calm, unhurried atmosphere en route.
▶ Make sure the child has plenty of fresh air.
▶ On coaches, sit above the centre of gravity.
▶ Older children will find it better sitting in the front of a car.
▶ Lie the child down on the back seat, if this is possible.
▶ Sickness can be worse in the morning, so schedule your journey for the afternoon or evening if you can easily do so.
▶ If travel sickness is severe, ask your doctor to prescribe a drug, and make sure that you give it to your child early enough.

Distraction
▶ Looking out of the front window at the horizon diminishes nausea. Play 'I-Spy' or road sign spotting games.
▶ Keep your children occupied, so there is no time for them to think about feeling sick.
▶ If possible stop, so that a child who is feeling sick can take a break for some air and a walk around.

Warning signs
▶ Older children will be able to tell you when they feel sick. With a younger child you should be suspicious if she falls silent, bursts into tears, looks unnaturally white, or her mouth starts to water.

Practicalities
▶ Certain snacks are better for sickness-prone children:
Apples
Dry biscuits
Glucose sweets
Crisps
Barley sugar
Iced water from a thermos, rather than fizzy drinks
Biscuits flavoured with ginger.
▶ Have a container such as a large plastic ice-cream tub or plastic bags for your child to be sick in.
▶ Have wipes or damp kitchen towels to clean her up.
▶ Give her sips of water afterwards, and a sweet to take away the taste.
▶ A damp cloth sprinkled with bicarbonate of soda will remove the worst of the smell.

(see box) and coaches are notoriously bumpy. Usually the going is slow, which is boring for the children, and they may find the seats uncomfortable. If the sun is beating through the window, draw the curtains for a while. You can also buy sun-shades that stick on to the window with suction pads.

If coach is your only option, and the operator accepts children, there are ways of making the journey easier. Make sure that you arrive early to claim good seats. Try to choose a 'luxury' coach that has its own loos, and that offers refreshments and video films. The better equipped the coach, the more the children and you will enjoy the journey. Superior coaches even have sleeper bunks for particularly long journeys.

Keep everything that you need for the journey close by – wash bag, change of clothes, snacks and games – otherwise you may find your luggage inaccessibly stacked behind everyone else's in the luggage hold.

TRAVELLING BY FERRY

A ferry has many of the advantages of the train, although children prone to travel sickness may suffer badly if the sea is at all rough. Space can be at a premium at busy times and it may be worth booking a cabin, especially if the journey is going to take any longer than two hours. Many parents advocate a night crossing and suggest that, if you are driving, you get your children into their pyjamas before you leave home, so that they can sleep in the car and be carried to the cabin when you board the ferry. It is also worth choosing the crossing that brings you closest to your destination, even if it is more expensive.

Remember to have a small bag packed with everything you might need during the crossing, and to take it with you, as you may not be able to get access to your car during the trip (see All You Need for Your Journey, page 38).

If you have a day-time journey, all but the travel-sick are likely to enjoy it. Children can run around and make as much noise as they like on deck – about the only form of travel where this is possible. Some ferries have videos for children, and some have a playroom too. There are also a lot of tempting slot-machines, so you may want to steer your older children away from them. If the communal areas around the bars are very busy, with long queues, you may consider it money well spent to have a sit-down meal in the restaurant.

Almost all major ferry companies provide mother and baby areas, where you can feed and change the baby in relative privacy.

TOP TEN TRAVEL PASTIMES

Games in which you can all participate make the time on a journey go faster, and help to distract anyone who is feeling sick or miserable. The sillier the game the better, usually; avoid competitive games with children who get too serious about them.

▶ I Spy
Even non-spellers can enjoy the game if you play it by nominating the *sound* the word starts with.

▶ Song and story tapes
If you have a cassette player in your car this can help to pass time very pleasantly. Use the song tapes when you are feeling energetic, or when you want to raise spirits, and sing along too. Story tapes can be used for quieter, more reflective times. If your children have personal stereos they can listen to tapes of their own choice without disturbing others, and they can be used on trains, ferries, coaches or planes as well as cars.

▶ Silly sentences
Children who can read can join you in making silly sentences from the letters on car number plates. J E S – John Eats Skyscrapers. This doesn't have to be competitive as it is fun in itself, though you can give points for the silliest sentence, or the first one to be thought of, if you like.

▶ Car spotting
Award points for different kinds of vehicle: one for a Mini Metro, two for a Rolls Royce, three for a fire engine, four for a motorbike with side-car, and so on. Choose vehicles your children know and give the more unusual ones the highest points.

▶ Legs
Count the legs on pub signs: two for The Duke of Cambridge, twenty-two for The Cricketers, and none for The King's Head! Rather than see who can spot the signs first, children can take the ones on the side on which they are sitting.

▶ Aunt Tabitha
A memory game. You start off 'Aunt Tabitha went to Paris and she bought a toothbrush'. The next person repeats the sentence and adds another object, and so on – until someone makes a mistake in the list. For added fun, make Aunt Tabitha's destination the same as your own. Children may like to call her by the name of someone they know – like the head teacher – and make the objects she buys increasingly ludicrous.

▶ The holiday song
Choose an easy tune that you can all sing, and make up words about yourselves and the holiday. They don't have to be clever, or rhyme, to make this fun.

▶ Eggs, bacon, chips and peas
When all reading matter has been exhausted on a long train, ferry or coach trip, or your flight has been delayed, this game can be played with any book or newspaper. Read a passage, but substitute words that begin with E, B, C and P with the words eggs, bacon, chips and peas – or other silly words.

▶ The alphabet game
A subject is chosen, such as names, countries, food, cars, types of building, and everyone has to think of an example beginning with A. When no more can be thought of you move on to B and then C, etc.

▶ Twenty questions
One of you chooses to be a person or an object, and the others must try to guess who or what they are by asking questions that can be answered with a 'yes' or a 'no'. If it is not guessed by the twentieth question, the chooser is the winner.

SAFETY ON HOLIDAY

It is ironic that most accidents happen in the home, yet people tend to worry most about personal safety when they are travelling and when they are abroad. The explanation is probably simple: when you are worrying, you are vigilant, and when you are on your own territory you relax and feel sure that nothing bad can happen. It certainly *is* better to worry, if worrying means that you take more sensible safety precautions.

It takes time for children to learn what is dangerous and what is not, and at home you are constantly teaching your child what is safe through daily repetition of 'no' and simple explanations. Inevitably, in an unfamiliar environment your younger children will not have this useful background knowledge about what they can or cannot do. Just because a child has learnt not to touch an electrical socket at home, it does not mean that he can yet make the mental leap to realize that a very different looking foreign socket is dangerous too. Increased vigilance is necessary to protect even sensible older children from inadvertently getting into danger.

At the stage when you were planning your holiday, you will have found out a lot about your destination and its possible dangers, particularly if you were going abroad (see Planning, page 16). But do remember that going to another part of Britain, in a strange place, your children can also be confronted with hidden pitfalls, both indoors and out. Your accommodation, where you will be spending much of the time, can present problems and must be made as safe as possible.

TRAVELLING

Be sensible about obeying all safety rules to the letter. In a car, keep your children restrained in child seats or by harnesses or seat belts. Do not let children put their heads or arms out of the window of a car, a coach or a train. On board a ferry keep your eye on them at all times, especially on the deck, when older, boisterous children may try to climb the rails. And watch out for younger children near stairs and in the crush at the bars and shops. When on a plane read the illuminated signs and obey instructions about staying in your seat and wearing seat belts.

▶ *See page 23 for Before You Go*

AT YOUR DESTINATION

Road sense
Holiday high spirits may make a child temporarily forget common sense on roads. Abroad, they may also be confused by the fact that the traffic is on the 'wrong' side of the road. If children become separated from you while abroad they may be doubly frightened by the fact that they cannot make themselves understood. Make sure they stay near you all the time, and use reins on young children.

In the country
Make it a strict rule that children should never eat berries without checking first with you whether they are edible. Keep an eye on little ones to see that they do not eat any tempting-looking leaves, flowers or berries. Don't let children wander into fields alone where there may be crops or animals, and always close gates after you. On country roads, remember always to walk facing the on-coming traffic, and make your children walk on the inside of you, and behind you when a vehicle approaches.

Animal sense
Teach children to be wary of *all* strange animals and never to stroke or pet an animal they do not know. These rules are even more important on the continent where the possibility of the animal having rabies is a real one.

Water safety
A small child can drown in only a few inches of water, so very young children must be watched all the time when they are near water.

It is sensible to teach children to swim as soon as possible, so that they know about breath-control in the water and are not panicked by getting water in their eyes or up their nose. But do not assume that just because your child can swim a little he is automatically safe. Being able to swim quite well in a pool does not prepare a child for the currents of the sea, or the waves when it is windy, or falling into water fully clothed. Even strong adult swimmers can get into trouble – the more confident the swimmer, the more risks he is likely to take.

It is sensible to take the following precautions:

- Do not let your children play alone on an inflatable mattress or boat; currents can pull them far out before they know it. Always attach a rope to such playthings and tether them or hold on to the rope.
- Give a nervous non-swimmer or learner a rubber ring or armbands. But do remember that these only help to keep their heads above water and are not safety aids in the way a lifejacket is.
- Only let your children dive once you have ascertained that this is completely safe. Hidden rocks, or water shallower than it looks can cause serious injury.
- Everyone should wear lifejackets when in a boat.
- Always check with the locals or holiday rep about all aspects of the local waters. You need to know the pattern of the tides, how quickly the water becomes deep and what, if any, the danger spots are.
- Always pay attention to warning flags, and make sure that you know what they mean.
- Make your children wait at least an hour after eating before they go into the water. Swimming diverts the blood away from the stomach and into the muscles, possibly resulting in cramp, which can put a swimmer in danger.
- If there are sea urchins or other nasty creatures lurking in rock pools, children can protect their feet by wearing plastic shoes.

YOUR ACCOMMODATION

You are unlikely to find that the place where you are staying is totally safe for small children. One of your first jobs must be to check the accommodation and equipment and do your best to make it as safe as possible, if necessary by improvising.

Ask about the safety of the local water if you are abroad. If there is any doubt, buy bottled water to drink.

SELF-CATERING

All the rooms in your villa, cottage or apartment must be checked from the point of view of security, but especially the kitchen area, which can be the most hazardous of all.

- The furniture in rented accommodation can be old and unstable. Rickety tables should be moved to a spot where crawlers and climbers cannot use them for support. It might be worth taking along some table corner protectors.
- Rugs on tiled or wooden floors can be very slippery. If your child is unsteady on his feet, it would be best to roll them up.

- ▶ If the fires are in use they *must* be guarded. Whether it is in use or not, make sure that a gas or electric fire is not easy for a child to turn on. Disconnect the plug if it is electric or securely tape the gas tap.
- ▶ Find a high place to store cleaning materials and bleaches or tether the cupboard doors together with string.

HOTELS AND SELF-CATERING

- ▶ Windows are a danger to an exploring young child. If a window does not have bars, move furniture away from it so that a child cannot easily climb up to it, or secure it with string so that it cannot be opened wide enough for him to crawl out.
- ▶ Examine balconies carefully. If you think a child could crawl through the bars, ask to be moved to the ground floor or make a webbing by criss-crossing the bars with string so that your child is unable to get through the gaps.
- ▶ Plate glass can be a danger to children who may run into it, not realizing it is there. Stick some masking tape crosses over it.
- ▶ Light switches on the continent are usually set at lower levels, and sockets are often in tempting positions. Make sure that your children learn quickly that they should not be touched, and use masking tape to cover up socket holes if necessary.

Cots

If a cot is provided, check it over to see that it is quite safe. If not you may decide that a bed, despite its drawbacks, would be safer.

- ▶ Check there are no loose screws or holes in the base, which would make it unstable.
- ▶ Look out for dangerous fittings such as wooden or metal knobs or loose screws which might catch clothing or scratch skin.
- ▶ The cot should be deep enough to stop your baby being able to climb out.
- ▶ See that the gap between the mattress base and bottom rail is no more than 2.5cm (1in), or children could get hands or feet stuck.

Beds

- ▶ Bunk beds should have a safety rail on the upper bed. But check that there is not too big a gap between this and the mattress, or a child may be able to slip his body through, but not his head, and in that position it is possible for him to get caught and choke.

Lifts

- ▶ Check that the lifts are safe if your children are old enough to work them by themselves. Three-sided lifts are dangerous for children.

HEALTH AND FIRST AID

It may seem unlucky to think about getting ill on holiday – but you are far more likely to cope well if you have given it some thought beforehand. While only a very few of you will spend time laid up incapacitated, you will be extremely unusual and lucky not to suffer one of the host of minor ailments that seem to go with being on holiday: a nasty insect bite, a day or two of holiday tummy, or the after-effects of spending too much time in the sun.

A medical problem always seems worse while you are on holiday and far from home, away from the surgery of your local doctor. It can be particularly nerve-racking when you are in a foreign country and do not speak the language. And after all, you are supposed to be enjoying yourselves, not feeling ill, or having to nurse the sick! However, you and your children are extremely unlikely to get anything seriously wrong with you while you are on holiday, and if you are sensible and well-prepared you should be able to deal quickly and effectively with any of the minor emergencies that may arise.

Precautions start here. If you are going abroad you may need vaccinations, and you must take a first aid box. It makes good sense, also, to find out where the nearest doctor is when you first arrive at your holiday destination. If you are holidaying in Britain and need to see a doctor, you can register with any local G.P. as a temporary resident and will be treated in the normal way.

VACCINATIONS

Make sure that you are protected against major illness by having the correct vaccinations administered before you go. When booking a holiday abroad, or soon after, you should check what is likely to be necessary. The best person to ask is your doctor, who is kept informed on the immunization requirements of foreign countries, and will know if a recent outbreak of anything serious means that you need to be inoculated before you go. The DHSS produce a booklet called *Protect Your Health Abroad* (SA35) which gives general rules and lists of the countries that require immunization of tourists.

Check what immunizations you must have at least two months before you need to travel so that you and your children can be given the necessary injections in plenty of time before you leave. The injections are most effective when spread out over time – but if you have left it late, you should start the course of injections anyway, as some protection is better than nothing at all.

Doctors do not recommend immunizing babies under one year against typhoid, cholera and yellow fever, so you will have to postpone holidays to areas that require these until your baby is older. It is also suggested that you do not take a baby abroad until she has started her routine immunization courses against diphtheria, tetanus and polio. The three-part programme will have been completed by the end of the child's first year, and a booster inoculation is given at the age of five. It is important to make sure that your child has this booster: tetanus is a serious illness caused by dirt getting into open wounds, which is a particular hazard if you are on holiday in the country or on a farm. If your child does sustain a dirty injury while on holiday and has not had a booster in the last five years, take her to a local doctor: the tetanus booster can still be reasonably effective if given retrospectively.

▶ *See page 60 for First Aid Kit*

THE DANGER OF THE SUN

Many people choosing a summer holiday abroad can't wait to expose themselves to the welcome heat after the chilly damp of Britain. But too much sun is bad for you, and can be painful and dangerous for babies and young children who are unaccustomed to it. The sun is at its most powerful in the middle of the day, and it is sensible to keep your children out of the sun at this time throughout your holiday. If you are allowing them to stay up later in the evenings with you, it would be sensible to let them take a nap after lunch, as continental children do, which means they will naturally miss the harshest rays from the sun. Late afternoon is the best time of all to be exposed to the sun, while the rays are cooling. Early morning rays are also more benign, but the danger is that you may not notice the gradual heating up as the day wears on, and may therefore allow your children to take more sun than is good for them.

A baby under six months has skin too delicate to be exposed to the sun at any time and her internal cooling system is not efficient enough to deal with the direct heat. Keep babies of this age covered up in light cotton clothing and a full-brimmed sun hat. Try to make sure that the pushchair or carrycot is in a place that is warm but in the shade, preferably with a slight breeze so that the baby does not overheat. For additional protection fit a sunshade to the pushchair. Use the highest protection-factor sun cream on your baby's skin.

Older babies and young children can be allowed a certain amount of sun, though if you don't want them to suffer you should only allow them to expose themselves for a short time each day until they build up an immunity. No more than five minutes is recommended on the first day, but you can double the amount of time each day thereafter. Try to find a pleasant play area in the shade so that your child doesn't feel too deprived by not being able to sit in the sun, but remember that the sun's rays can bounce off bright sand and water and continue to burn even when your child is in the shade.

Timing their exposure to the sun is the only way to protect your children. The problem is that they won't know when they've had enough sun as sunburn has a delayed reaction. A child may feel perfectly all right after taking too much sun, but will suffer some hours later. The tell-tale sign is reddening of the skin, but even this is not immediately apparent when the sun is bright.

Apply high-factor protective sun cream on your children at least every three hours, and always after swimming, when it is likely to have washed off. The 'protection factor' tells you how long a child is allowed to stay in the sun without burning. A protection factor of 'four' allows her to stay out in the sun four times longer than she could if she were unprotected. Use the highest protection-factor sun cream that you can buy for infants and small children – this is currently fifteen.

Do not let your children play unclothed for long in the sun, until they are accustomed to it. Insist that they wear a floppy sun hat and are covered up by a long-sleeved shirt made of light Indian cotton and a pair of shorts. These will give quite good protection, and can even be worn while swimming – the hot sun dries them in minutes afterwards. Plastic sandals will protect children's feet against the burning sand, and can be used to paddle in pebbly waters. They can be quickly wiped dry afterwards so that your child's feet do not slip inside them.

Remember that in a hot climate your children are likely to lose much more fluid as they run around and sweat. See that they have plenty to drink – particularly small babies who may only be able to signal that they are thirsty by crying. It is handy to take water with you on to the beach so that you don't spend a fortune on commercially produced drinks. Keep it cool in a flask if possible.

SUNBURN

Sometimes, despite your best efforts, your children get sunburnt. This is most likely on a blustery day, when the wind has a cooling effect on the skin, so it is only when it is too late that your child notices that her skin is hot and burning and she is miserably uncomfortable. The more fair-skinned your child the more easily this can happen with even the smallest overdose of sun. Red-headed and blonde children are most likely to burn in the sun.

The symptoms are obvious, and include:
- ▶ Bright red, painful skin
- ▶ Skin that is very sensitive to the touch, so that even a light sheet feels heavy and uncomfortable, and the skin itches
- ▶ This is later followed by the surface skin drying and peeling in white flakes.

The best way to deal with a sunburnt child is as follows:
- ▶ Keep her indoors until the skin loses its redness and stops hurting. Outside, even in the shade, the child will still be getting a certain amount of the sun's rays as they bounce off sand or water.
- ▶ Give cool baths or showers to soothe her overheated skin.
- ▶ Use calamine or other creams specifically formulated for sunburn to help cool her skin.
- ▶ A mixture of vinegar and water sponged on to the skin is a cheap way of cooling inflamed parts.

HEAT STROKE AND HEAT EXHAUSTION

Much more rarely, over-dosing of the sun can lead to heat stroke, caused by excessive sweating and the unhealthy loss of fluids and salts from the body. These are the main symptoms:

- ▶ Unusual tiredness
- ▶ Bad and persistent headaches
- ▶ Sickness and nausea
- ▶ Skin that is cold and clammy to the touch.

The treatment is usually simple:

- ▶ Move the sufferer into a cool place and give constant sips of a drink. You can either use rehydrating sachets mixed with water (see First Aid Kit, page 60) or get her to sip plenty of drinks, ideally some boiled water mixed with salt, to the ratio of half a teaspoon to one pint (half a litre).
- ▶ If the symptoms persist, see a doctor.

SNOW CARE

- ▶ It is possible to get sunburnt when skiing too, even when it is cold. Remember to apply sun cream to your children with as much care on the ski-slopes as on the beach in summer. A total sunblock, which does not allow your child to tan at all, is probably best.
- ▶ The glare reflecting up from the snow is much brighter than the sun on a bright day at the beach. This light is bad for the eyes, and small babies should be kept well protected from the glare; children should wear goggles.
- ▶ Even when it is not sunny your children's skin needs protection from the cold and wind with a good moisturizer, otherwise their skin will get chapped.

BITES AND STINGS

Bites and stings are rarely dangerous, though they can be extremely uncomfortable and distressing to children, particularly the bites that continue to itch for days.

Gnats, midges and mosquitoes usually attack at night.

- ▶ A sure defence is to keep your children completely covered up in long-sleeved and long-legged pyjamas, though they are adept at finding any exposed flesh, such as toes and hands or face and neck.
- ▶ They can also be kept at bay by insect-repellent sprays, which you should spray round their bedroom when you put the children to bed.
- ▶ A more efficient alternative is a mosquito coil which you light at night and which gives off a smell that the creatures find offensive –

unfortunately, so do some people!
- ▶ A more expensive, but equally effective, electric gadget heats up insect-repelling tablets, which do not give off such an unpleasant smell.
- ▶ Also very effective are insect-repellent gels that can be rubbed lightly into the skin in the evening and again at bedtime.
- ▶ If your child gets bitten, apply pieces of ice, or an ice-cold bottle to the sting to soothe the area, and use calamine lotion to reduce the itchiness to some extent.

Bee and wasps can attack in Britain as well as abroad.
- ▶ Scratch out the bee sting with your clean fingernail.
- ▶ Ice-cold compresses or a specially formulated cooling spray will help calm the sting.
- ▶ Vinegar and calamine lotion also soothe wasp stings.

Jellyfish barbs can continue to sting for a long time.
- ▶ Use wet sand to rub the barbs off.
- ▶ Apply ice or hold a cold compress or an ice-cold bottle to the affected area.
- ▶ The irritation can be eased by antihistamine preparations.

Sea urchins are to be found lurking on beaches and in rock pools. If you know they are about, you should encourage your child to wear plastic shoes while paddling. If trodden on, the sea urchin's long black spines break off and become embedded in your child's foot, causing great pain.
- ▶ If this happens, buy some magnesium sulphate from a chemist. A paste of this, when applied to the foot, will help bring the spines to the surface.

CALL THE DOCTOR IF...

- ▶ First aid and home remedies do not bring relief when they should.
- ▶ Your child's reaction seems to be allergic rather than normal.
- ▶ A bee or wasp sting is on or in the mouth.
- ▶ Your child is bitten or scratched by a stray dog or cat while abroad, because of the danger of rabies.
- ▶ After a jellyfish sting your child faints or becomes notably short of breath.

Try to find an English-speaking doctor for these or any other emergencies so that you can be sure the doctor knows exactly what happened and any relevant facts about the child's medical history. Alternatively, if you are on a package holiday and there is a courier on duty who speaks the language, ask to be accompanied to the doctor.

DRINKING WATER

Find out in advance whether the drinking water in the area you are visiting is safe. Travel companies and locals are usually frank about this. If the water is not safe, or is suspect, these are the precautions you should take:

- ▶ Never drink water straight from the tap.
- ▶ Boil the water for five minutes before drinking it or using it to make up your baby's bottle. If you are bottle-feeding and will need to do this a number of times a day, a portable boiler will be a useful piece of equipment.
- ▶ At other times make sure you buy bottled water. Children usually prefer still mineral water to the sparkling variety. If you can find water with a low mineral content, this is better for babies.
- ▶ If buying still mineral water in a bar or restaurant make sure that they bring the bottle unopened to the table, or there is a risk that they have merely filled it from the tap.
- ▶ If boiling is impracticable, use sterilizing tablets in the water. They have a taste many children dislike, so you may have to add flavour with squash.
- ▶ Remember to keep a bottle of mineral water for cleaning teeth too.
- ▶ Do not use the tap water to wash fruit or salads.
- ▶ Do not put ice in your drinks.

FOOD POISONING

If you have been warned by your travel agent or doctor that the water is unsafe, then you will probably have to be alert about general food hygiene.

- ▶ Avoid freshly made ice-creams; instead buy the famous brands that are produced and packed in sterile conditions in a factory.
- ▶ Watch out for ready-cooked food that has been left out for a long time uncovered and attracting flies.
- ▶ It is better only to eat fruit and vegetables that have been cooked, unless they are peeled or thoroughly washed in safe water.
- ▶ Avoid shellfish.
- ▶ Do not eat food that has obviously been made in advance and reheated.
- ▶ Bear in mind that unboiled milk is unlikely to be safe unless it is pasteurized or is a long-life variety.
- ▶ If the sea seems contaminated, resist the temptation to swim in it.
- ▶ Get your children into the habit of always washing their hands after they have been to the loo.

STOMACH UPSETS

Even if you have been scrupulously careful and clean in your habits, it is still possible that one of your children will pick up a stomach complaint of some sort. There is, however, no need to worry if any of you are suffering from slight constipation, or are simply moving your bowels more frequently than usual. Changes in food and routine on holiday often have this effect and do not mean anything is wrong.

Stomach upsets can usually be treated by you without calling the doctor or giving medicines:

- ▶ Replacing the lost fluid is the most important thing. Fizzy drinks that have lost their sparkle are good for children: you can make them flat by adding sugar. Or give a pinch of salt and a teaspoon of sugar in a tumbler of water.
- ▶ If you have brought any of the sachets that prevent dehydration when mixed with water, give these (see First Aid Kit, page 60).
- ▶ Do not give milk drinks or milk products.

CALL THE DOCTOR IF...

- ▶ A baby becomes obviously dehydrated, with a dry tongue, excessive drowsiness and a consistently dry nappy.
- ▶ A baby under six months has severe diarrhoea for more than half a day.
- ▶ A child under the age of three has severe diarrhoea for between twelve and twenty-four hours, particularly if accompanied by vomiting.
- ▶ A child between three and twelve has severe diarrhoea for two days, or moderate diarrhoea for three days.
- ▶ A child under five has a high temperature (38°C or 101°F) for more than twenty-four hours.
- ▶ There are other symptoms, such as persistent abdominal pain for more than four hours, blood in the motions, or if the child constantly vomits.
- ▶ A vomiting child has other symptoms of illness, particularly persistent abdominal pain or headache, or blood in the vomit.

After the crisis has passed:

- ▶ When your child is feeling better, increase food intake slowly, but continue to withhold milk products.
- ▶ Dry biscuits, plain boiled rice or apple purée are good first foods after a stomach upset.
- ▶ Respect it when your child indicates an instinctive dislike of certain food – this reaction can be a sign that it may not agree with her.

FIRST AID KIT

You can buy first aid boxes ready packed, though it is probably cheaper to make one up yourself and stock it with the preparations you know you need and prefer. You can use a sturdy plastic box, and tape a cross with red sticky tape on it so that it is easily identifiable. This is a list of basics:

- Antiseptic, such as T.C.P.
- Sticking plasters
- Junior paracetamol or other pain-killing syrup
- Antiseptic cream and wipes
- Zinc and castor oil cream for soothing sore babies' bottoms
- Cotton wool
- Rehydrating sachets such as Dioralyte or Rehidrat (a sugar/salt/glucose mix to be added to boiled water for your child to drink during a stomach upset)
- Travel sickness pills appropriate for the age of your children – get a prescription from the doctor
- Pain-relieving spray for bites and stings, such as Waspeze
- Gum-soothing gel for a teething baby
- Calamine lotion for soothing burns or bites
- Sunburn cream
- Vitamin drops
- Any medicines your doctor has prescribed for your child

Also useful:
- Scissors
- Safety pins
- Sterile dressing
- Bandage
- Non-mercury thermometer

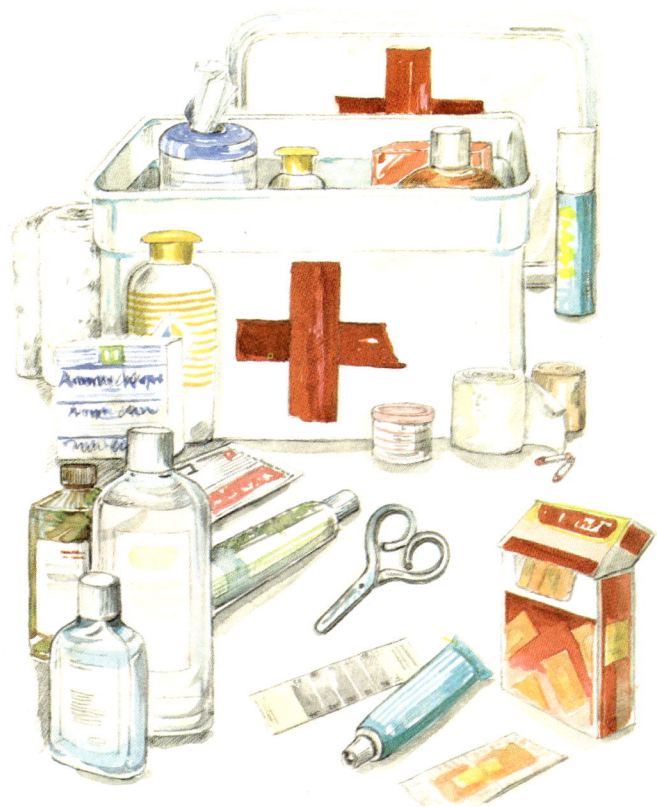

HEALTH AND FIRST AID

MEDICAL CARE

You are usually entitled to free or reduced price health care when travelling to most European countries, New Zealand or Hong Kong. To know how these arrangements work, get hold of the DHSS leaflet SA36, 'How to get medical treatment in other European Community countries', and SA30, 'Medical costs abroad'. This includes the application form CM1 which you should fill in before you go abroad to receive Form E111, which you must show to the foreign doctor or hospital when you have treatment.

This arrangement is not quite as good as it sounds. Some doctors will refuse to treat you under the scheme, and those that do may only give cursory treatment. You usually have to pay for the treatment first and claim money back when you return home, and even then you may not get all your money back – particularly if costs incurred include ambulance charges and hospital accommodation. Neither are the costs of getting back to this country, if illness has caused you to miss your flight, given back to you. Examine the leaflets carefully to see which conditions or illnesses are excluded.

PRIVATE INSURANCE

Because of the pitfalls of this scheme you are wise to seek the protection of a good private insurance policy. You may be offered one when you book your holiday, or you could ask a local insurance broker. Otherwise any travel agent will be able to arrange this for you. Choose the best scheme you can afford. A matter of a few pounds extra can mean thousands saved if one of you needs to go to hospital.

Choose a policy:
▶ with at least £50,000 worth of medical cover for Europe and £500,000 worth for North America
▶ that offers a 24-hour English-speaking telephone service to put your mind at rest
▶ that will pay your costs back to this country if necessary
▶ that pays for additional hotel or other expenses for healthy members of the family to stay near a sick relative
▶ that pays your bills direct, rather than reimburses you later
▶ that leaves you free to use the doctor or hospital of your choice
▶ that reimburses all your expenses in the event of cancellation, and covers loss or theft of your possessions.

▶ *See page 23 for holiday insurance*

USEFUL ADDRESSES

Air Transport Users Committee
c/o CAA
45–59 Kingsway
London WC2B 6TE
(01) 242 3882
Produces a free booklet for air travellers, with a section on babies, and a leaflet for first-time fliers.

Air Travel Advisory Bureau
320 Regent Street
London W1R 5AE
(01) 636 5000
Provides information on cheapest and most convenient flights to any given destination.

Association of British Travel Agents
55–57 Newman Street
London W1P 4AH
(01) 637 2444
Publishes a leaflet outlining their services, which include advice on all aspects of travel.

Automobile Association
Fanum House
Basingstoke
Hants. RG21 2EA
(0256) 20123
Publishes guides to different types of holiday and offers members advice on route planning.

British Activity Holiday Association
Rock Park
Llandrindod Wells
Powys
Wales LD1 6AE
(0597) 3902

Camping and Caravanning Club Ltd of Great Britain
11 Lower Grosvenor Place
London SW1W 0EY
(01) 828 1012

Caravan Club
East Grinstead House
East Grinstead
West Sussex
RH19 1UA
(0342) 26944

English Tourist Board
Thames Tower
Black's Road
London W6 9EL
(01) 846 9000

Irish Tourist Board
150 New Bond Street
London W1Y 0AQ
(01) 493 3201

National Association of Holiday Centres
10 Bolton Street
London W1Y 8AU
(01) 499 8000

Northern Ireland Tourist Board
River House
48 High Street
Belfast
BT1 2DS
(0232) 246609

Scottish Tourist Board
23 Ravelston Terrace
Edinburgh
EH4 3EU
(031) 332 2433

Ski Club of Great Britain
118 Eaton Square
London SW1W 9AF
(01) 245 1033

Wales Tourist Board
8–14 Bridge Street
Cardiff
CF1 2EE
(0222) 227281

INDEX

A
Activity holidays 6, 15
  see also Skiing
*Agent's Hotel
  Gazetteer* 18
Air travel:
  airport facilities 40–1
  amusing children 34,
    40, 42, 48
  boarding early 40,
    41
  choosing seat 40
  feeding babies 42
  getting to airport 23
  hand luggage 35–6
  meals 36
  night flights 40
  pressure changes
    42
  safety rules 49
Alphabet game, the 48
Animals 50, 57
Apartments, rented
  see Self-catering
  holidays
Armbands 51
'Aunt Tabitha' 48

B
Babies:
  bottlefeeding 23, 26,
    33, 58
  and car journeys 43
  feeding 23, 26
  heating food for 30
  holiday checklist 25
  kit for journey 32
Baby-sitting services 9,
  21
Bags *see* Luggage
Balconies 21, 52
Baths:
  baby 29
  in hotels 21
Beach *see* Seaside
Bee stings 57
Bibs 30
Bites:
  dog or cat 57
  insect 56–7
  spray for 60
Boats, inflatable 51
Booking holidays 16–
  22
Booster seats 30
Bottlefeeding 23, 26,
  30, 33, 58
Brochures, holiday 17–
  18
Bunk beds 52

C
Camping 6, 9–10
  booking site 18, 19–
    20, 22
Car, hiring a 32
Car journeys:
  amusing children 34,
    40, 44, 48
  babies on 43
  clothes 32, 36, 39
  food 33, 44
  loading the car 36,
    43
  at night 42
  safety rules 49
  toddlers on 44
  using Motorail 42
  see also Travel
    sickness
Car spotting 48
Caravans 6, 9–10
  booking sites 18, 19–
    20, 22
Carriers, baby 29
Cat scratches 57
Cholera immunization
  53
City holidays (abroad)
  6, 12
Clean-ups 32
Clothes:
  for cold weather 27
  for hot weather 26,
    54, 55
  for journeys 32, 36,
    39
  packing 24, 25
Coach travel 46–7
  clothes 32, 39
  games and toys, 34,
    40, 44, 48
  luggage 37–8, 47
  see also Travel
    sickness
Cots 17, 20, 52
  see also Travel cots
Cottages, country *see*
  Self-catering
  holidays
Countryside:
  hotels abroad 6, 12
  safety rules 50
Cycling holidays 15

D
Dehydration 56, 59
Diarrhoea 59
Doctors 53, 57, 59
Dogs 50, 57
Drinking water 58

Drinks for journeys 33,
  44

E
'Eggs, bacon, chips
  and peas' 48

F
Ferries 47
  food 38
  luggage 38, 47
  safety rules 49
First aid kits 34, 60
Food:
  on aeroplanes 36, 42
  for babies 23, 26
  for car journeys 33,
    44
  dislike of 59
  on ferries 38
  hygiene abroad 58
  on trains 37
Food heaters 30
Food poisoning 59

G
Games for journeys 48
Gnats 56–7

H
Harnesses, safety 28,
  35
Heat exhaustion, Heat
  stroke 56
Highchairs 30
Hiring a car 23
Holiday camps, British
  6, 13
Hotels:
  abroad 6, 11–13
  baby-sitting services
    21
  baths 21
  booking 17–18, 19,
    20–1
  British 6, 9
  meals 20, 21
  safety precautions 52
House-swapping 6, 14

I
Immunization *see*
  Vaccinations
Insects:
  bites 57
  repellants 56–7

Insurance, holiday 23, 61
Inventories 21
'I Spy' 48

J
Jellyfish stings 57

L
Lifts, hotel 52
Light switches, continental 52
Luggage 24, 31–2
  for air travel 35–6
  for car journeys 36
  for coach journeys 37–8, 47
  on ferries 38, 47
  packing 25
  for train journeys 37

M
Meals:
  hotel 20, 21
  see also Food
Medical insurance 23, 61
Midges 56–7
Mineral water 58
Money for emergencies 23
Mosquitoes 56–7
Motorail journeys 42
Motorway service stations 43
Mugs, trainer 30

N
Nappies 24, 26, 32
Nappy-changing:
  on aeroplanes 36
  on car journeys 43
  on trains 45
Nappy-changing bags 29
Night driving 42
Night-lights 29

O
Overnight stops 32

P
Package hotels see Hotels
Packing 24, 25
Passports 23
Planning holidays 6, 16
  involving children in 23
Plate-glass 52
Pony-trekking 15
Potties 29
Pushchairs 28, 35

R
Rehydrating sachets 60
Reins 35
Renting cottages see Self-catering holidays
Road sense 50
Rubber rings 51
Rucksacks, children's 25, *31*, 32

S
Sailing holidays 15
  water safety 50–1
School, missing 16
Sea urchins 51, 57
Seaside holidays:
  booking 19–20
  checklist for 26
  package hotel abroad 6, 11
  safety rules 50–1
  see also Sun and Sunburn
Self-catering holidays:
  abroad 6, 7–8, 17
  booking 18, 19, 20, 21–2
  in Britain 6, 7, 17
  checklist 27
  safety precautions 51–2
  sharing accommodation 16
'Silly sentences' 48
Skiing holidays 15
  clothes for 27
  snow care 56
Sockets, electrical 49, 52
Stereos, personal 44, 48
Sterilizing tablets 58
Stings:
  bees and wasps 57
  jellyfish 57
  spray for 60
Stomach upsets 59

Suitcases see Luggage
Sun, protection from 54–5
Sunburn 55
Suncreams 54, 55
Swimming 50, 51

T
Table seats, foldaway 30
Tapes, story 48
Tetanus immunization 53
Toddlers 16
  and car journeys 44
  getting about with 35
Toys for journeys 34, 40, 44, 48
Train journeys 45
  food 45
  games and toys 34, 40, 43, 44, 48
  luggage 37
  nappy-changing 45
  restaurant cars 45
Trainer mugs 30
Travel agents 17–19
Travel cots 23, 29
Travel sickness 34
  on coaches 47
  coping with 46
'Twenty questions' 48
'Two-centre' holidays 12
Typhoid immunization 53

U
Upset stomach 59

V
Vaccinations 23, 53
Vomiting 59

W
Wasp stings 57
Water, drinking 58
Water safety 50–1
Which? magazine 18

Y
Yellow fever immunization 53